Beautiful
GARDENS
of Britain

EXCALIBUR BOOKS

Published in the United States by
Excalibur Books, 201 Park Avenue South,
New York, NY 10003.

Not to be sold outside of USA and
its territories

© Marshall Cavendish Limited 1978

Printed in Great Britain

ISBN 0 525 70260 1

Contents

GARDENS:
an introduction

The development of gardening in Europe was fairly late by world standards. In far away China, gardening was a craft in ancient times and, although there is evidence of gardening on Crete and in ancient Egypt, we do not really begin to learn about plants and gardening in Europe until the campaigns of Alexander the Great (356–323 BC) which brought the Greeks into contact with Asia.

Most of this information comes from the writings of Theophrastus, popularly called the father of botany, who made use of the information brought back by the learned men who travelled with the armies of Alexander. In addition to the mass of description, his was the first serious attempt to classify the vast plant world. Further, his will shows that he had what would now be called a botanic garden. This he left to some of his friends so that they might continue to use it for study. The art and craft of garden design, however, does not seem to have been as highly developed by the Greeks, as it was soon to be by the Romans. Two early authors give us a great deal of information about the plants and gardens of Rome at about the time of the coming of Christianity. Pliny the naturalist (AD 23–79) produced his *Historia Naturalis* which included the natural history of plants, while his nephew, Pliny the younger, was a writer and orator, and it is from his letters that we learn about the design of Roman gardens.

From the uncle we learn that the range of plants had increased since the time of Theophrastus – for example, a red rose was now in cultivation. The gardens described by the nephew were architectural and formal, the ancestors of the great gardens of the Italian Renaissance. They were also similar to the gardens built by

Gardening had been a well-established art in many areas of the world long before it was widely practised in Europe. Below: An eighteenth century Indian painting depicts the sophisticated design of a formal Indian garden.

the Romans when they occupied the British Isles - an example of which, at Fishbourne, Chichester, has been uncovered.

The younger Pliny's garden in Tuscany stood high up with a view to the Appenine mountains. It was almost an extension to the rooms of the house, reached through a portico, in front of which was a terrace adorned by statuary. There was much box cut into fancy shapes, an open air dining room, a marble summer house, a fountain throwing water high into the air, while plane trees gave shade.

At about the same time that Pliny the elder wrote his natural history, another learned man Pedanios Dioscorides, produced his famous *Herbal*. This was concerned with the medicinal value of plants. And for centuries to come, the study of plant-life, which later developed into the science of botany, was devoted almost entirely to these medicinal uses. With the rise of Christianity and the development of the monastic orders, the so-called flower gardens were devoted almost entirely to producing plants of alleged medicinal value: Dioscorides' book was for centuries the standard work.

The Moslem world inherited much of the knowledge of classical civilization. For a period, Persian gardening and garden design was of a high standard. Through Persia, too, along the great silk road, passed many trees and plants from the ancient horticulture of China, such as the mulberry and peach, on their way to Europe.

Much information about gardening exists from the medieval period in Europe. Some of it is to be found in the increasing number of herbals that were published, some in poetry, such as the *Romance of the Rose* which was translated into English by Chaucer, and a great deal in the exquisite illustrations of day to day life and common objects that adorn the so-called *Book of Hours*.

These pictures show us the medieval gardens. Invariably they were small by modern standards, walled and safely enclosed from the perils of the outer world, with elaborate fountains and carved seats. There is close-clipped topiary. The flower-beds are small and laid out in geometrical patterns called knots. Within the safety of their walls the owners and their friends sit about singing and playing,

Above left: Detail from a Roman fresco for the Casa di Livia worked at the time of Christ. The Romans inherited much of their knowledge of gardening from the Greeks and greatly developed it.
Above: The remains of the Roman garden uncovered at Fishbourne near Chichester.

Right: It was with the Renaissance that the gardens in Europe developed to a hitherto unknown magnificence. The gardens of the Villa d'Este in Italy are a surviving example of the splendour of this period.

or making love – all dressed in their finery. Occasionally, recognised by his sober clothing, a gardener is seen going about his work. Garden tools were heavy and clumsy – spades were of wood, shod with iron.

No comparable pictures of gardens in the British Isles exist, and it is generally assumed that its castle and private gardens were not nearly so advanced as those on the Continent.

Our monastery gardens are, however, far better described and, on account of the close contacts between the monastic orders of Britain and the Continent, were very similar to them. Their principal objective was the cultivation of plants having medicinal value.

There is plenty of evidence concerning the vegetables cultivated in medieval times. Plants such as the potato were, of course, unknown and most of the plants consumed were little better than those that grew naturally wild but were presumably a little more tasty from being carefully cultivated. Some fruit, such as figs and mulberries, seem to have been quite early introductions, while the vine was also grown here at least from Roman times.

A great development in both horticulture and particularly garden design came about with the Renaissance in Italy. Gardens of hitherto unknown magnificence, and of the finest architectural quality, were made. With the great developments of international trade, plants were introduced from one continent to another. While a commanding natural view was sought, the garden itself was full of artifice - superb statuary, ingenious fountains, terraces and flights of steps.

The movement and the style spread northwards as did the great increase in knowledge of plants and their cultivation. Their impact on England can be traced to about the time of Henry VIII's meeting with Francis I at the Field of the Cloth of Gold in 1520. Cardinal Wolsey at Hampton Court commissioned the first garden on a magnificent scale in the new manner (which the King took over)

and which the Tudor nobility emulated. Both garden design and the craft of horticulture, as well as the science of botany, developed at a phenomenal rate. Seafarers brought plants home from the temperate part of the world, particularly eastern North America. The same was happening in France from where introductions were brought over to Britain and bulbs from the Cape and plants from the Orient were often introduced through another great trading and horticulturally minded people, the Dutch.

In 1597 came John Gerard's *Herball*, largely cribbed from a work by the Belgian Dodoens, but full of his own observations on the novel plants now growing in England. Such were the South American tomato (first grown for decoration purposes) and the wrongly called African marigold from Mexico. This last was among the plunder brought back by the Spaniards when Cortez defeated the Mexicans in 1520. He found in South America that the art of gardening was an ancient one and highly developed, while the plant life was to provide us with many things, none more important that the potato which was first illustrated in England in Gerard's book. We can say that during the late sixteenth century the British first realised the extremely wide range of plants that could be grown, and became pre-eminent as a nation of plantsmen. This was signally shown in John Parkinson's *Paradisi in Sole Paradisus Terrestris* of 1629, which laid emphasis for the first time on the garden flowers 'admired for beauty' rather than on their use in medicine.

From now on gardens large and small were part of the British scene; their frequence and excellence – and, incidentally, the beauty of the mown grass – was remarked upon by travellers from abroad. More and more use was made of orangeries or conservatories to protect tender plants through the winter.

From now on the British Isles were in the main stream of international botany and horticulture, particularly when the first botanic garden at Oxford had opened

Above: Part of the gardens at Hampton Court. The first garden in Britain to be commissioned in the Renaissance style, it has been greatly changed over the centuries. However, in an attempt to re-create the atmosphere of the sixteenth-century gardens, part of the grounds have been restored to their original design.

in 1621 (the first, at Padua, was begun in 1543). British botanists and gardeners travelled abroad, and such distinguished foreigners as Clusius (1526-1609) visited Britain.

In the meantime, the impetus and originality of the Renaissance had rather faded from the Italian scene, and had been transferred to France, where the design of gardens had become more elaborate and grander in scope. A new spirit was showing in the work of designers such as J. A. du Cerceau (1510-1585). Finally, André le Nôtre (1613-1700) evolved a new style of the greatest magnificence, profoundly architectural and formal in character and in accordance with the splendour of the court of the 'Sun King', Louis XIV. During the Cromwellian period, the exiled court of Charles II saw this style of garden-making, which spread over Europe as far afield as Scandinavia and Russia. On the Restoration in 1660, it was brought to this country, and became the fashion. Two great gardeners, George London (who died in 1713) and Henry Wise (1653-1738) formed a partnership as garden designers and nurserymen - their site being near where the Victoria and Albert Museum stands today - and dominated both the design and planting of the gardens of the great. The fashion was for walled gardens with elaborately patterned beds, called parterres, formed both from plants and coloured gravels. They also made great use of clipped evergreens (topiary) which like avenues and other Dutch influences was associated with the arrival of William and Mary in 1688.

At this period, garden art and craft, as well as the study of botany, was surprisingly international in character and uniform throughout Europe and indeed beyond. It was in the hands of highly skilled professionals.

In the eighteenth century a revolution originating in England took place. Brought about by philosophers and literary people such as the poet Pope, the essayist Addison and the philosopher Shaftesbury, nature and irregularity was held to be the guiding light in garden design, particularly as seen in the Italian landscape paintings of Claude and Poussin.

The revolution in taste was violent. In the hands of William Kent, Lancelot 'Capability' Brown and Humphry Repton formality was ended; straight paths and avenues were destroyed, straight canals were turned into serpentined lakes and nature was triumphant. This style was to spread all over the world, and its freedom and apparent, yet carefully contrived, naturalness is still the key to much garden design.

At the same time, interest in the plants themselves and their cultivation increased. The origins of the Royal Botanic Gardens at Kew were laid in 1759 when Princess Augusta, widow of Frederick, Prince of Wales, with the help of the Earl of Bute, instituted a botanic garden in her private grounds there. This soon became the most important botanical garden in the world, and the British – particularly the Scots – were so skilled in the following decades that their services were sought all over the world.

The greatest influence on gardens and gardening during the nineteenth century – which continues to this day – was the rapid growth of an industrial, urban civilization whose members, as their income permitted, moved out into the suburbs or even the country. Many more people had gardens, and interest in horticulture was greatly increased. In Britain this was indicated by the foundation of what is now the Royal Horticultural Society in 1804, and the publication of the first gardening periodical, *The Gardener's Magazine* in 1826.

Two of the most important events at that period were when the Horticultural Society sent David Douglas (1798-1834) in 1824 to the Pacific coast of North America whence he brought back trees, shrubs and plants to Europe which made a revolutionary change in the plants cultivated. In 1843 the Society sent

Below: In contrast to the gardens of Britain which were moving towards a more 'natural' style, the gardens of the continent, such as these gardens at Château Villandry in the Loire valley, remained highly formalised.

Above: The improvement of greenhouses in the early nineteenth century greatly extended the varieties of plants which could be cultivated in Britain. The Great Palm House at Kew, built in 1848, was the most modern and the grandest of its day.

Robert Fortune (1812-80) to China; he, too, brought back plants which are now essential commonplaces in British gardens. Phillip von Siebold (1796-1866), physician-naturalist to the Dutch East India Company, likewise brought back a multitude of plants to Holland from Japan. And there were many other collectors, including the Russians, particularly in the areas across their eastern borders.

Early in the century greenhouses were improved. For long, they had been buildings of architectural merit. Now they became functional, and for the first time were heated successfully by the simple circulation of hot water. The great palm house at Kew (1848) was an example of this development.

A great era of plant-breeding and selection of good kinds began and although the scientific principles of this were not generally known until 1900, surprising successes were achieved, particularly by Continental nurserymen.

Towards the end of the century Britain made another contribution by the development of the woodland garden in which trees, shrubs and plants, particularly bulbs such as daffodils, were naturalised. This was a logical succession to the earlier landscape gardens. In them were grown the many trees and shrubs, particularly rhododendrons and magnolias, introduced from the remoter parts of Central and Western China. First made known in Europe by French missionaries, of whom Armand David (1826–1900) was the most outstanding, and English Customs officials, such as Augustine Henry (1857-1930), these were introduced by collectors, notably E. H. Wilson (1873-1932), J. F. Rock (1884-1962) – an American – and Reginald Farrer (1880-1920). To Farrer we also largely owe that very popular twentieth-century development, the alpine garden.

The Second World War accelerated many social changes. Except in North America, the large garden became an economic impossibility while small gardens multiplied. Of the estates of the gentry of the eighteenth and nineteenth centuries, some disappeared under redevelopment, while others were either taken over by the National Trust or opened up to the public by their owners in an attempt to preserve them. Most have been successful and today there are a variety of gardens open where the visitor can wander at his leisure for a relaxing afternoon or, for the more energetic and enthusiastic gardener, to pick up hints and tips on gardening for use in his own garden.

Alton Towers

The remarkable garden of Alton Towers, Staffordshire, hidden away in the picturesque valley of the little river Churnet, was created by the immensely rich Earl of
Shrewsbury in the opening years of the nineteenth century. He engaged celebrated
architects, whose designs, however, he himself often modified. Begun in 1814 and
added to by his successors, his fantastic garden remains almost unaltered today.

One of the most fascinating features of the garden is the wealth of buildings
and statuary on display At the head of the valley, below the lake, is a statue of
the earl within a small Grecian temple bearing the inscription: 'He made the desert
smile'. Nearby stands a romantically conceived imitation of Stonehenge and a
series of ornate conservatories within part of which is a stony grotto. To the
right of the valley stands a red building originally intended to be a 'harper's
cottage'.

An ornamental canal curves along the bottom of the steep valley, the sides
of which are interlaced by a network of paths and steps leading from viewpoint
to viewpoint and passing a rich variety of fantastic buildings, fountains, colonnades,
statuary and other garden ornaments. The trim lawns between are planted with
flower beds, particularly of roses, and there is a magnificent array of conifers and
other ornamental trees. But, it is in mid-June that the garden reaches the peak of
its beauty with great masses of flowers of the naturalised *Rhododendron ponticum* in
bloom.

However, an even more memorable sight is the exquisite Chinese pagoda
rising out of a pond from the top of which a fountain plays, watering the surrounding trees. The garden is beautifully kept and secluded from the other popular
features of the place. It can be viewed from an aerial railway.

Alton Towers is about a mile to the north of the well sign posted village of
Alton, off the B5032 road, five miles east of Cheadle.

*Below: A section of the garden in
summer with the conservatory in the
background. An integral part of the
garden design at Alton Towers, the
network of paths and steps lead the
visitor from one attractive feature of
the garden to another.*

9

Above: Secluded in the depths of the valley in which Alton Towers is situated, the elegant pagoda fountain rises from a pool and throws its fountain some sixty feet into the air.

Above right: The wide variety of garden buildings and ornaments at Alton Towers caused much criticism when the garden was first designed. However, as the gardens have matured, the ornaments have become a distinctive feature of the place.

Right: Alton Towers, now a ruin, seen across the lake with some of the fine specimen trees in the foreground.

Anglesey Abbey

The first Lord Fairhaven bought this old house in 1926 and made around it a garden on the grand scale, well suited to the flat Cambridgeshire landscape with its wide horizons and spacious sky-scapes. Great use is made of sweeping vistas through trees, together with smaller, more intimate areas which are planted to give colour at varying seasons of the year. The garden is furnished with distinguished statuary, some of which comes from the original great garden at Stowe in Buckinghamshire.

On the southern side of the house is the Rose Garden where the grey walls of the house provide an effective backdrop for the delicate colours of the roses. A short walk around the east end of the building and northwards lies the Herbaceous Garden with its original semi-circular plan.

From here, by working one's way across the end of the Aboretum, with its many rare trees, and passing the informal Quarry Pool, you reach the quarter mile Emperors' Walk where, against a background of dark and silver evergreens, are set twelve busts of Roman Emperors. Halfway down this walk, a turn to the right leads across the Aboretum to enter the South Glade, a sweep of grass with trees irregularly planted on either side. At the far end lies the start of the Coronation Avenue, planted in 1937. Straight as a die, four rows of planes and horse chestnuts on either side stretch for over half a mile. Intersecting this is a path which gives a surprise view of the Circular Temple, which is reached though a dark, bosky grove. It consists of a circle of large Corinthian columns guarded by two lions couchant. Turning right down another wide, glade-like lawn, one again reaches the house.

Seasonal features are the daffodils, the Hyacinth Garden and the Dahlia Garden. There is also a Pinetum.

Anglesey Abbey, a National Trust property, is six miles north-east of Cambridge on the B1102.

Left: The house at Anglesey Abbey seen across the wide sweeping lawn. Above: A ornate Chinese style temple containing a large porphyry bowl.

Much of Anglesey Abbey's original design was arranged around Lord Fairhaven's fine collection of statuary.
Right: The Circular Temple, a collection of Corinthian columns surrounded by a yew circle with a copy of the Bernini David in the centre.

Below: The Rose Garden lying to the south-west of the house, the walls of which act as a splendid foil to the bright colours of the flowers.

Antony House

In the late eighteenth century, Cornish gardeners found that their climate enabled them to grow, out of doors, a great many plants which, elsewhere in Britain, needed winter protection under glass. This led to a type of garden particularly associated with Cornwall. Usually made in Victorian times, by one of the old Cornish families, it incorporated both the remains of the old style and the beginnings of the new, using plant introductions of the later nineteenth and early twentieth centuries.

Antony Park, with its interesting interior, was built in the early eighteenth century for Sir William Carew. However, the garden is new, the work of Sir William's successor Sir John Carew Pole, and created in 1945.

The house stands above the tidal estuary of the River Lynher, which is seen at the end of vistas framed by giant ilex trees planted in 1760. Around the house are lawns and topiary, including an extraordinary giant cone in yew. In the broad alleyway is a large maidenhair tree – the ginko – a survivor from prehistoric times. Its remains are found as fossils, and it still grows wild in China.

The new part of the garden forms an arc centred upon the house. It is typical of the modern woodland type but is differentiated by the massing of shrubs and plants usually grown in small numbers. *Pieris forrestii*, whose flaming foliage in spring is as brilliant as any flower, is an example. The hybrid *williamsii* series of camellias, originated by J. C. Williams of Caerhays by using *C. saluenense*, introduced from western China as recently as 1924, as a parent, is also widely planted as are *Rhododendron cinnabarinum* and its hybrids with their bell-like pendant flowers ranging from red through rose to orange. There, too, are masses of the lilac-blue *R. augustinii* and the giant-flowered, heavily scented Loderii hybrids. Magnolias, viburnums, embothriums (the Chilean 'Fire Bush'), Crinodendrum with their crimson lantern-like flowers as well as maples and magnolias are steadily maturing year by year.

Antony House is a National Trust property, situated five miles west of Plymouth via the Torpoint car ferry.

Below left: The colonnaded entrance to the garden enhanced by the mature growth of climbing plants. Below: The remarkable yew 'arbour' clipped to the shape of a perfect cone.

Above: Charming painted statues of a shepherd and shepherdess dating from the mid-eighteenth century stand on either side of a garden seat in the tall closely clipped yew hedge.

Right: The Burmese temple bell, a trophy of the nineteenth century Burma wars, flanked by granite lanterns from Japan.

Ascott

Though set in typical English countryside with wide views sweeping over the Vale of Aylesbury, Ascott is not a typically English garden; it is more representative of the nineteenth century Continental style.

The ground is terraced so that the view is unobstructed and on one terrace, called the Madeira Walk, the shelter is used to protect tender plants. On the lawns around the house we first notice one of the main features of the garden – the presence of many variegated and coloured-leaved forms of trees and shrubs. From this upper level the clever and extensive use of clipped evergreens to form compartments can also be seen one of which has, at its centre, a rather baroque fountain set simply in the grass.

Elsewhere is a remarkable garden in the nineteenth century French style. From a small pond of geometric design, surrounded by a gay parterre, rises a fountain from a base of dolphins that epitomises the last century.

Around it is topiary cut into cork-screws and other odd shapes. Another remarkable example of topiary will also be noticed – a sundial, spread out on a lawn, whose gnomon and hours are all cut from living evergreens.

On the other side of the house is an informal lily pool with its borders well-planted with trees and shrubs in a typically English manner.

In spring there is colour from many Japanese Cherries and massed bulbs that are naturalised.

Ascott is a National Trust property lying ½ mile east of Wing, two miles southwest of Leighton Buzzard on the south side of A418. Opening times vary from year to year.

Overleaf: The lead fountain of Venus in a shell chariot is surrounded by a clipped Golden yew hedge and a well-kept circular lawn.

Below right: The summer house at Ascott. Approached along a gravel walk, the colourful borders are always filled with seasonal planting. Below: A feature of the whole garden at Ascott is the colour contrasts in the trees and shrubs and there are many clipped evergreens.

Ashridge

A community has existed at Ashridge, Hertfordshire, since the thirteenth century when it was a monastery. After the dissolution of the monasteries, it became a royal residence. The present building dates from 1815 and to the south of it there is a level garden with numerous interesting features.

Humphry Repton carried out much work at Ashridge and is reputed to have made seventeen smaller gardens within the whole to break up the rather level overall effect. A few of these gardens remain. There is, for instance, the Monks'

Left: The grey stone buildings at Ashridge not only contrast with the other local buildings, they also provide an excellent foil for the colour of the trees and shrubs.

Below: The conservatory fronted by a lovely showing of rhododendrons and flowery borders.

Above: The terrace close to the house is treated formally with clipped yews and small box-edged beds.

Above right: The Monk's Garden was designed by Humphry Repton who carried out much work at Ashridge. This garden is next to the old cloisters of the Monk's Barn and forms a secluded and peaceful part of the main garden.

garden, which consists of a parterre surrounding a cast iron monument (recently restored). The Monks' Barn runs along one side of this garden and is divided from it by a herbaceous border. There is too, a circular rose garden surrounded by a high hedge, and also a small garden with wisterias trained as standards in front of a conservatory. The orangery has now become an integral part of the building and forms a perfect background for the small Italian garden with central fountain and fish pool. The massed planting of rhododendrons lends colour across the lawn.

A unique feature of the garden is an immense square skating pond formerly flooded in winter, now with steps leading down to the paved base. Two tree-houses or arbours nearby are unusual. Their fernery and grotto made of Hertford-shire pudding stone were added in the nineteenth century and the tunnel beyond may well have been an old ice house. To the west an avenue of Liquidambar trees planted in 1936 leads along the extremity of the garden to a hard-to-find Bible Garden – containing a small stone carving of an open Bible.

Amid the grounds of the extensive Ashridge Park, administered by the National Trust, the garden itself is owned by the Ashridge Managements Committee, the building being used as a college. It is situated on an escarpment in the Chiltern Hills, four miles north of Berkhamsted, and can be approached by a toll road from either Berkhamsted or Little Gaddesden.

Athelhampton

Dorset abounds in fine Tudor houses and Athelhampton ranks with the best. It is fortunate that in the late nineteenth century it was given a garden which matches it so perfectly that it is difficult to realise it was made 300 years after the house was completed. This harmony is partly a matter of style, partly of material, a major part of the garden having been designed as a series of formal enclosures with pavilions, terraces and walls built of Ham stone similar to that used for the house. There are two quite large rectangular gardens and two smaller ones with a circle, or corona, in the centre from which each of the others can be reached.

Long vistas have been preserved through these gardens both from north to south and from east to west but the full character and beauty of each can be seen only by entering it. There is much fine stone and iron work, several fountains and pools and a great deal of well-kept topiary, some grown to great size. One of the larger gardens is backed by a high stone terrace with flanking stone pavilions and from this some of the finest views of garden and house can be obtained.

Below: A beautifully enclosed circular pool at Athelhampton, from which point radiate various walks to other parts of the garden.

Above: One of the many long vistas through the gardens with statuary in the foreground.
Above right: Some of the large topiary specimens with the Tudor building in the background.
Right: A waterfall and a riverside walk, the banks planted with water-loving plants and overhung by trees.

The little River Piddle almost encircles Athelhampton and from the formal gardens a path leads beside the river to a very different series of gardens to the west of the house. Here the dominant feature is an ancient dove-cot standing in a large lawn and backed by a yew alley which leads diagonally back to the river. Behind this alley are well-stocked herbaceous borders and the old reed-thatched stables. A little stream crosses the lawn and its banks are planted with moisture loving plants with shrub roses beyond. Development is continuing at the present time, especially in the improvement of the river-side garden.

Athelhampton is situated one mile east of Puddletown on A35.

Belton House

Belton House, Lincolnshire, home of the Brownlow family for 300 years, is one of the finest Wren-style houses built in Britain during the Restoration period in the seventeenth century and, as the house stands on the slopes of a limestone escarpment, the garden has no affinity at all with the flat, bleak fenlands that form a large part of Lincolnshire.

The estate covers well over 600 acres. Massive and mature trees sweep in the form of a great avenue over the escarpment.

The gardens next to the house are formal. Northwards from the terrace, which has many steps, there is a fine view down an avenue of yews. The tall columnar yews are flanked by lawns with roses in box-edged parterres terminated by two half-circular, box-edged lawns.

Left: A view overlooking the formal Italianate garden at Belton House showing the clear lines of its flower beds and clipped trees.

Below left: A curved wall with a dripping fountain and pelargoniums grown in pots set in the wall niches. Below: Decorative wrought iron gates and screens leading to the stable block.

Above: The orangery or camellia house, with the ancient village church on the right.

A Cedar of Lebanon standing alone leads the eye gently to the great lawn and to a fountain and round pond setting off a classical-styled orangery, now a tea-house decorated with growing camellias.

At Belton the ancient village church forms a pleasing part of the landscape to the right of the orangery. In spite of changes, many features at Belton recall the eighteenth-century landscape tradition, including the gothic ruin near the stables, a dried-up canal, a temple, a noble-looking sundial with figures of Father Time and Cupid and the magnificent avenue of trees leading from the east up the hillside to the Bellmount tower (1750) which consists of a giant arch capped by an upper storey.

To the south-east and east the park and woodlands in the distance are landscaped in the style of Lancelot ('Capability') Brown.

Belton is 2½ miles north-east of Grantham-Lincoln A607 road.

Bicton

The gardens at Bicton consist of three distinct areas, the so-called Italian Garden, the American Garden and the Pinetum.

The first is said to have been designed in the style of Le Nôtre in the eighteenth century. It is still formal in design, with a rectangular pool, a fountain and a canal, but now Victorian in character, with its dominating Deodars and other conifers. Above it, at one end, stands the range of glasshouses with a Temple at their centre, and, somewhat detached, the handsome Palm House. These contain a most interesting range of plants all clearly labelled.

From this range of houses a good view is obtained of the formal lay-out while to the left of it is the American garden for which there was a vogue early in the last century in which were grown many trees, shrubs and plants, introduced from North America. Here too there is much to see all the year round with many fine specimens including the rare Mexican or Montezuma Pine as well as rhododendrons and azaleas in the spring.

The Pinetum, originally laid out in 1830 and subsequently added to, particularly in 1910 when many of the then new introductions from western China were added, contains one of the most remarkable collections of conifers in the British

Below: The focal point of the formal gardens at Bicton, The Temple, set at the centre of a row of glasshouses, each of which contains an interesting range of plants all clearly labelled.

Above: The elegant fountain set in the centre of the pool in the formal gardens.

Right: One of the outstanding features in the Pinetum is the long avenue of Monkey Puzzels (Araucarias) planted in 1844.

Isles. Among its sombre shades are majestic specimens of record size and rarities seldom grown elsewhere in Britain.

Beyond the Pinetum lies the Hermitage, a nineteenth century summer house covered with wooden shingles, the floor made from the knuckle-bones of deer. Delightful views of the gardens and particularly the Pinetum can be had by taking a trip on the 18 inch gauge railway.

Bicton Gardens are at East Budleigh, two and a half miles north of Budleigh Salterton on A376.

Blenheim

The original garden at Blenheim was begun in 1705, designed by Henry Wise, gardener to Queen Anne, around the magnificent Palace designed by Sir John Vanbrugh, for John Churchill, 1st Duke of Marlborough. This garden consisted of a parterre near the house and a kitchen garden some way off. The parterre was in the baroque style, still to be seen in gardens in France, Germany and Austria, but nowhere else in the British Isles. It was laid out in swirling scroll-like patterns, studded with small bushes clipped into geometrical shapes. Leading away from the house there are long, tree-lined vistas, crossed by Vanbrugh's triumphal arches.

Towards the end of the eighteenth century, fashion in garden design swung away from formality and 'Capability' Brown in 1746 transformed the steep-sided valley by damming the little river Glyme to make the present great lake, one of the finest sheets of artificial water in Europe. The slopes of the valley were handsomely planted with trees in the style of the mid-eighteenth century.

Alas, at this time the great parterre was destroyed, but to replace this the 9th Duke of Marlborough, in 1925, employed a French master of the old formal school, Achille Duchêne, to re-plan it and thus give some idea of the original setting of the Palace. Duchêne ably complied with this and created formal gardens with ponds, fountains and parterres – one of the major delights of Blenheim and reminiscent of Versailles.

Blenheim Palace, with its extensive garden and surrounding parkland, lies in the village of Woodstock, eight miles north of Oxford on the A34.

Overleaf: One of the Bernini fountains in the Water Garden.

Below left: Although much of Blenheim is laid out in the 'natural' style of 'Capability' Brown, the grounds nearest the Palace have been restored to a style more fitting to the age and design of the house. Below: The meeting point of the two styles of garden design: the bridge was designed by the foremost architect of the eighteenth century, John Vanburgh, over a canal – later extended into an artificial lake by 'Capability' Brown.

Bodnant

The garden at Bodnant, near Conwy in North Wales, has been described as 'the finest of contemporary British gardens'. It is renowned all over the world and visited by tens of thousands of people each year. Its development was begun nearly a century ago, and was continued by the first Lady Aberconway and her son, the 2nd Lord Aberconway, who gave the garden to the National Trust in 1949.

Bodnant is now the home of the 3rd Lord Aberconway who is president of the Royal Horticultural Society. The whole garden covers nearly 90 acres and like many fine gardens is made up of a number of smaller ones. Around the house, and on the hillside immediately below, there are six great terraces, designed in the Italianate style, with lawns, pools, rose gardens, great trees and other features such as garden statuary and urns.

The terrace walls and the pergolas are clothed with plants many of them rare, others tender but flourishing in this mild, moist climate.

On the canal terrace at one end of a long, narrow, formal pool stands the Pin Mill, originally built about 1730 at Woodchester in Gloucestershire. It was once used for pin manufacture, hence its name, but was moved to its present site just

Above: The view looking southwest over Bodnant's Italianate terraces and the formal Lily pool (The Lily Terrace) to the Snowdon range.

Left: A glimpse of the woodland garden, developed in the glen, full of bright colour in May.

Above: The Pin Mill, originally used for pin manufacture in Gloucestershire, at the end of the canal, seen from the open air theatre.

before the last war and is now used as a garden house. At the other end of the canal is an open-air theatre built in the Italianate style.

Leading from the terraces, there are walks lined with rhododendrons for which Bodnant is famous, with camellias and with flowering trees. They take you to shrub gardens and down to the glory of this garden, the Dell. This is a glen in which tower many fine specimen trees, especially conifers, many of them planted nearly a century ago and through which runs the little river Hiraethlyn, its power once used to turn a flour mill. From a bridge which spans the river there are fine views along the Dell.

The banks are planted with masses of rhododendrons, particularly of the azalea section, camellias, enkianthus and other shrubs. Round the rocky pools, there are primulas and other moisture-loving plants.

Bodnant is on the east side of the Conwy Valley some four miles south of Conway and seven miles from Llandudno and Colwyn Bay. It is seven miles north of Llanrwst, on the A470 (A496) road. Visitors are admitted only at the main entrance on the Eglwysbach road, where there is a car park.

The garden is supervised by Lord Aberconway, V.M.H. for the National Trust.

Borde Hill

Borde Hill is a delightful stone-built Sussex manor house standing on a low saddle of ground a little to the north of Haywards Heath. The original garden is in the landscape style with a large lawn to the south terminated by a deep ha-ha (a dry ditch with a vertical face on the side of the lawn), permitting uninterrupted views towards the South Downs and, to the north, an entrance drive with a little terraced garden below it, which equally effectively displays the rolling, well-wooded countryside in that direction. The southern vista is flanked by trees which extend to form a woodland where the ground rises and then falls into two large dells, perhaps the sites of medieval mining operations.

Into this lovely setting a notable collection of choice plants has been introduced during the present century. Rhododendrons fill the formal beds in the terrace garden beside the drive and flank the path leading to the woodland. They also fill large parts of the woodland itself and the larger of the two dells, in the shelter of which they have grown very large. Great drifts of highly-coloured azaleas ring the main lawn and grow on the lower slopes of the woodland. At its highest point, where there is another smaller house with a little garden of its own, half-hidden in the trees and bushes, there are raised stone-edged beds and a somewhat formal design, though the whole is so heavily clothed with anthemis and other hardy plants that its formal character is almost concealed.

The second of the two dells has been developed as a water and bog garden. Here will be found the Ostrich Plume and other hardy ferns together with hostas, irises, astilbes, euphorbias, ligularias and many more plants with fine foliage to supplement their flowers.

The garden is reached on the Balcombe road over one mile north of Haywards Heath.

Below: The stone-built manor house at Borde Hill in its beautiful setting.

Above: A statue by the Italian sculptor, Antonio Tantardini, of a veiled woman.
Right: Azaleas are quite a feature of the garden and the 'Azalea Ring' is outstandingly lovely in May.

Right: Near the walled garden, where there are examples of camellias 'Donation' and 'Salutation', there is some fine topiary work.

Bramham

Why is it that Britain has no great formal gardens, architecturally designed, elaborated with terraces, canals, fountains, temples and long straight vistas on the same scale as those of Italy, France, Spain, Austria and elsewhere on the Continent? The answer is that in the early eighteenth century the English landscape garden was developed and fashion decreed that all the old gardens should be replaced by those in the new style of 'Capability' Brown. All went, except a very few that were somehow overlooked; one of these is the delightful Bramham Park, Yorkshire.

Robert Benson, later Lord Bingley, in about 1699 acquired the estate upon which Thomas Archer designed a house. Around this the garden was laid out. First came the long, straight woodland walks and the formal canals to which, up to about 1750, the buildings and ornaments were by degrees added.

The whole plan was devised in the form of simple geometry. At one point where rides intersect stands a magnificent vase, the 'Four Faces', from which there are views down a canal and up the long 'Cathedral Ride'. At one end of the broad walk in front of the house is a temple in the Ionic manner from which there is a view in retrospect to the obelisk pond, from which water pours down an elaborate cascade. A delightful octagonal 'Gothic' temple provides a view which includes the pond seen from another aspect. There are, too, carefully designed vistas over the park.

The trees, mostly beech, between which these walks passed, had become huge, their smooth grey trunks majestic. In February 1962 a devastating gale blew about 400 right over, their roots tearing up the ground. Many others were damaged. With great courage, the owners began clearing the wreckage, and then to replant. The young trees have grown well.

Bramham Park lies six miles south of Wetherby just off the A1 road.

Below: One of the canals at Bramham, one of the few original formal gardens remaining in Britain.

Above: The octagonal 'Gothic' temple, one of a number of fine garden buildings at Bramham Park. Above right: One of the grotesque wall fountains through which water is fed into the canals.

Right: The entrance gates, flanked by sphinxes and elaborate rustic piers.

Branklyn

Branklyn is a remarkable garden, as exciting for the plantsman as it is for the amateur. The size of the garden is now two acres. In 1926 when the late John and Dorothy Renton built the house it was about a third of the size and contained but few plants and those of no great outstanding interest. It was some years before they became keenly interested, but their subsequent enthusiasm led to the gradual acquisition of an adjoining orchard until necessity or discretion called a halt when the garden had reached its present size. The things which interested them most were alpines and ericaceous plants. To accommodate these, two large scree beds were made and in due course peat walls in the shadier parts of the garden for the many gaultherias, cassiopes, vacciniums, dwarf rhododendrons and a multitude of other plants which prefer these conditions. In dealing with a small area the selection of plants is particularly important. At Branklyn each plant had to earn itself a place; rarity or cultural difficulty alone did not qualify. The same care in selection was applied to the trees and shrubs which now provide background and screening for the garden. They also contribute much to the atmosphere, which is further enhanced by a number of old apple and pear trees through which ramble roses and clematis and a notable plant of *Hydrangea petiolaris*. Where you have a choice visit the garden in late May, June or July when the majority of alpines are in flower and when meconopsis, iris, rhododendrons and lilies are at their best. The majority of shrubs and trees flower well during these months, although hoherias, hydrangeas, shrub roses and of course herbaceous plants continue well into August.

When Mr and Mrs Renton died, the property was offered in the will of John Renton to The National Trust for Scotland, in whose care it now rests.

Branklyn is within the City of Perth. It lies on the east side of the River Tay a quarter of a mile south of Queen's Bridge on the Dundee road – one of the many gardens that flourish on the 'cold', east side of Scotland.

Below: Grass is used for the paths at Branklyn, running between borders richly planted with shrubs and perennials.

Above: The collection of plants amassed at Branklyn is remarkably wide, and all are peat loving. The garden was built up during the life-time of Mr and Mrs Renton and on their death given over to the National Trust for Scotland.

Right: A number of old trees have been enveloped in roses and clematis and add to the background colour effect of the garden.

Brodick

The Isle of Arran lies in the Firth of Clyde. It is mountainous – Goat Fell rises to over 2,800 feet – though the low ground by the sea is very fertile and the Gulf Stream gives mild conditions counter-balanced by destructive winds.

By the sea on the eastern side stands Brodick Castle, a typical Scottish baronial building with mountains as a back-drop. Immediately in front of the building there is a long grass terrace with magnificent views. This leads to an old walled garden containing six rectangular lawns between which are pergolas covered with wisteria and a good selection of climbing roses. Against three of its sides are borders of herbaceous plants as well as, for example, tender fuchsia hybrids.

Below that, separated from the sea by giant bushes of *Rhododendron ponticum* which give protection against storms, is a woodland walk.

In the thirty years before her death in 1957, the Duchess of Montrose cleared and converted ancient scrub to create the famous garden we see now. Bays were cleared to shelter the sensationally large-leaved and tree-like rhododendrons, many of which were introduced from western China and Tibet by collectors such as Forrest and Kingdon-Ward. With an annual rainfall of some 70 inches a year, these giants are so at home that they seed themselves.

More recently a rock and water garden have been added and even more rhododendrons introduced from the collection of Sir James Horlick on the island of Gigha. Brodick also boasts flowering trees and shrubs of all kinds, a 30-foot hedge of crinodendron, drifts of primulas of many kinds and meconopsis in blue, yellow and pink, and water-loving irises.

Brodick Castle and its 60 acres of garden are now in the care of the National Trust for Scotland. Ferry services run from Ardrossan and Fairlie to Arran and there is a bus service to the castle gates.

Below left: In spring the primulas make a wonderful display of colour. Below: The ameliorating effect of the warm Gulf Stream on the high altitude and destructive winds allows many tender plants to flourish.

Right: Brodick Castle is a typical Scottish baronial building, standing high on the Isle of Arran.

Below: The present garden was created by the Duchess of Montrose and upon her death in 1957 the estate was given to the National Trust for Scotland. The rock and water garden have been made since that time and many varieties of rhododendrons introduced.

Burford House

Burford House on the boundary of Shropshire and Worcestershire, is in one of the most fertile parts of Britain, watered by the River Teme after it has left the border of Wales. The river flows past the garden. An early eighteenth century red-brick building, Burford House is the home of Mr John Treasure, who has made around it one of the most original and interesting of modern gardens.

It is essentially a plantsman's garden in which the contents must have great decorative value rather than botanical interest. Around the house there is a raised area treated formally. The planning of the garden itself consists of irregularly shaped beds set in wide areas of mown grass. These beds are planted, as is the whole garden, with most carefully selected shrubs and plants. Foliage and form are as important as flower, while labour-saving is very carefully considered. Many plants are grown in an unorthodox manner – for example, clematis (of which there is a remarkable selection) are often found interweaving through other plants instead of being conventionally trained. The garden and its planting is of particular practical interest to those making small or moderate sized gardens.

Burford House lies off the Worcester–Ludlow A456 road, one mile west of Tenbury Wells and nine miles east of Ludlow.

Left: The eighteenth century manor house at Burford is set in one of the most interesting of modern gardens. The canal pool on the north side of the house reflects the only formality in the garden.

Below: The church tower set beyond the shrub borders. There is a good collection of shrubs now reaching maturity.

Below left: The paved garden and pool where the only splash of colour is provided by the petunias in plant containers.

Above: The decorative use to which many plants have been put in this garden makes it one of the most interesting for plantsmen to visit. Here ivy is used to clothe the steps that break up the levels of the garden.

Right: Part of the stream garden at Burford House, a garden that makes full use of the water from the River Teme that runs through it.

Buscot Park

Buscot Park, Berkshire, is a fine example of the work of Harold Ainsworth Peto, who continued the work of William Robinson and Gertrude Jekyll in breaking away from the stuffy, over-formal style of Victorian gardening.

Peto was one of the foremost garden designers, who developed a new style of simplified classical naturalness and understood the art of planting as well as design. It was William Robinson and Gertrude Jekyll who by their example and writings brought informal gardening with herbaceous borders and naturalised plants back into vogue.

In 1787, Buscot Park was merely a 'modern' house on a hill top with a 'pretty piece of water'. Peto, who lived from 1854 to 1933, showed his genius in using the lake to make a fine water garden. The principal feature which he created is a long grass walk with a narrow canal at its centre between high trees falling in a series of stages towards the lake. The lake presents a breath-taking vista as it suddenly appears in view.

The walk by the canal is full of varied interest. At one stage there is a fountain, and at another the canal is crossed by a bridge. The canal is planted with water-lilies and at the main intersection there are fine vistas crossing the main one.

Later additions to Peto's work include a young avenue of Cypress Oaks and a group of figures – examples of modern sculpture.

Buscot Park is a National Trust property and lies three miles north-west of Faringdon on the A417 Lechlade-Faringdon road.

The principle feature of Buscot Park is the long grass walk with a narrow canal at its centre. Left: The fountain at the top of the canal walk, leads down in a series of levels to the 20 acre lake below.

Above: Fine vistas cross the main one which runs the length of the canal and are framed by well-sited trees.

Right: Water plays a major part in the garden design at Buscot Park. Here the courtyard pool reflects the statues set in niches.

Castle Howard

Horace Walpole, the eighteenth century connoisseur, described Castle Howard, Yorkshire, and its surroundings, as 'sublime'. The woods he said, were worthy of being each a metropolis of the Druids. The lawn, he called the 'noblest in the world'. Begun in 1699, for Charles, third Earl of Carlisle, by Sir John Vanbrugh, the architect and dramatist, and Nicholas Hawksmoor, the architect, the building is surrounded by the first great landscape garden in the British Isles. It is quite distinct from the largest of the formal gardens of its day, but differs greatly from the typical 'Capability' Brown landscapes that followed.

The original long terrace extends from the east end of the house with giant statues spaced out along its route. It terminates in Vanbrugh's 'Temple of the Four Winds'; beyond lies Hawksmoor's mausoleum – two landscape garden buildings probably as beautiful as anything in Europe. Walpole wrote of the mausoleum that it would 'tempt one to be buried alive'. Below lies the lake. There are other objects of architectural interest, including a bridge, which leads the eye across the park.

Close against the house to the south is a simple formal garden with clipped hedges and statuary. In the centre is a large fountain with a Victorian style statue depicting Atlas supporting the globe. Other sculpture is well placed in the vicinity of the house, including a boar in the garden against the west side. Some delightful flower borders have recently been added.

Castle Howard is reached by passing through magnificent avenues of trees lying just north of the A64 road, six miles west of Malton and fourteen miles north-east of York.

Left: The view looking across the lake towards the 'Mausoleum'. Many of the gardens buildings were designed to form focal points for the views.

Above: The classical landscape as seen from near the 'Temple'. The bridge was designed by D. Garrett in the 1740s and the 'Mausoleum' by architect and dramatist, Nicholas Hawksmoor in the 1730s.

Right: The 'Temple of the Four Winds' designed by Sir John Vanburgh between 1724–26.

Charlecote

This estate belonged to the Lucy family from the twelfth century until it was given to the National Trust in 1945; the cleft oak palings which today surround the Deer Park and can be seen from the road, are of the type that has been used since medieval times.

While walking down the long straight drive leading to the Gatehouse, the visitor will see the well-stocked park, full of red and fallow deer which Shakespeare is supposed to have poached, and the herd of Spanish sheep. Over the years the brickwork of the Gatehouse has mellowed to a rosy pink and is unaltered since Shakespearean days. The Gatehouse leads into the forecourt with herbaceous borders and two charming lead figures of a shepherd and shepherdess dating back to 1718.

Over the chimney-piece in the Drawing Room an item of interest to gardeners can be seen. It is a fine painting of Charlecote in 1696 showing the formal garden which was swept away by 'Capability' Brown when he landscaped the Park about 1760.

The long Grass Walks within a walled garden, the elaborate parterres and the curiously designed Double Canal from which arose a tall summer house reached by a long narrow path with water on either side, have disappeared. The gardens by the house today, except for 'Capability's' Lebanon Cedars that sweep the grass, are of the nineteenth century, reaching down to the River Avon. All around are views of parkland which might well be the setting for a Shakespeare comedy.

Charlecote is four miles east of Stratford-on-Avon, on the north side of B4086. Bus 518 (Stratford, Warwick, Leamington, Coventry) passes the gate. The nearest railway station is Stratford on Avon.

Below: Balustraded steps lead down to the River Avon which meanders lazily through ihe park at Charlecote.

Right: The exquisite statue of a shepherd set against the red–bricked Tudor gatehouse.

Below: A shepherd and his dog and a shepherdess flank stone steps, the walls surmounted by flower-filled vases.

Chartwell

It is interesting to compare the garden around Chartwell created by Sir Winston Churchill, with that of his great ancestor, Marlborough at Blenheim Palace. The palace gardens at Blenheim are among the great and lavish spectacles of British gardens.

The magnificence of Chartwell is of another kind. It belongs to the wide and very English panorama of the countryside over which it looks.

The house is set towards the head of a steepish valley. It is unusually tall, looking back, in design, more to the English yeoman's home rather than the classical splendours of Blenheim. It stands on a platform which is irregularly terraced with some formality before merging into the landscape.

The entrance from the car park passes by some rock-work with a small pool, shrubs and trees. Below the house there are pools in the valley supplied by a stream. They are the fish pond, whose golden orfe Sir Winston delighted to see, the swimming pool and the waters on which glide the famous black swans, originally a present from Australia. All these are carefully landscaped into the scene.

The garden proper lies around the house, whose height and walls are well used to shelter climbing and other plants. There are steps down to the grass below, but it is better to continue along the higher level through a series of interlinked gardens, moving on as the view over the countryside, of orchards, fields and copses reaches out further and further. The most interesting part in high summer is undoubtedly what is now a large rose garden surrounded by the wall built by Sir Winston himself. Here is the walk of golden roses given to Sir Winston and Lady Churchill by their family as a golden wedding present.

Above: An ornamental vine scrambles over a pergola to give a play of light and shade.

It is pleasant to walk back on the grass immediately under the house. Good use has been made of the lower terrace walls, while in the grass there are planted a number of interesting trees, such as a yellow-flowered horse-chestnut (*Aesculus octandra*) and silver maples (*Acer saccharinum*) natives of North America.

Chartwell is a National Trust property. It is two miles south of Westerham, in Kent, forking left off the B2026 after one and a half miles.

Left: One of the outstanding features of Chartwell in summer is the sheltered Rose Garden.

Above: A view across the stream to the lawns and rose covered wall that surrounds the house just visible in amongst the trees.

Right: The rose garden in which the gold and yellow roses contrast splendidly with the blue of Nepeta mussinii planted around the edges.

Chatsworth

At Chatsworth, the ancient seat of the Dukes of Devonshire, is to be seen a history of gardening. The present house was begun in 1687. Around it, George London and Henry Wise, the most important garden designers of the day, laid out a vast and sumptuous garden in the style that Le Nôtre used for Versailles. Its elaborate design, lying among the sombre, remote hills, amazed travellers. Traces of this garden and its fountains still exist, particularly the grand cascade (a slightly later addition) that tumbles down the hillside. Next came 'Capability' Brown, who swept much of this away in the vogue for the natural landscape – and a lovely scene he devised in the park.

Chatsworth's great day was the arrival of an unknown young man on a spring day in 1826. The 'Bachelor Duke' had chosen him at a moment's notice to become head gardener. This was the first step to fame of Sir Joseph Paxton, later to design the Crystal Palace, based on the giant conservatory he built at Chatsworth for the Duke, which was demolished after the First World War. Much else of Paxton's work remains: there is his Emperor Fountain, throwing a jet 276 feet high; the camellia house – still looking 'modern' today and with some of the original camellias he planted growing within; there is his rock garden with its giant boulders and his arboretum with its many fine old trees surviving. Everything he did was on the most magnificent scale.

Today, we find also beds of roses, herbaceous plants and trees and shrubs of the latest kinds, all faultlessly cultivated, in addition to this historic gardening surviving from the past. A tour of the gardens, entailing a pleasant walk of something over a mile, takes one from the Orangery past the colourful borders and the Sea Horse and Emperor Fountains, into the Azalea Dell, at its best in late spring, thence through the Ravine and into the Pinetum. The path continues past various ponds to the Arboretum and on to the Cascade House. From here it winds through the woods back to the house. At various points one can diverge to see the site of the Great Conservatory and other features of this historic garden.

Chatsworth lies a little way East of the village of Edensor, six miles North of Matlock, on A623.

Left: The narrow glass fruit cases designed by Joseph Paxton in the nineteenth century.

Right: The Cascade House from which the Great Cascade emanates is one of the few pieces of the garden design of London and Wise remaining at Chatsworth.

Below: The spectacular view from the Cascade House to the bottom of the steep staircase.

Chilham Castle

Chilham Castle, near Canterbury, Kent, is built on the site of an ancient fort said to have been built by the Romans around 55BC. The octagonal keep of a later castle, Norman in origin, stands nearby in its own secluded garden. However, the existing fine red-brick manor house, around which the remarkable garden was designed, is of a much later period, Jacobean, and completed in 1616.

The main gardens consist of a series of terraces connected by flights of brick stairs, with long, flower-filled borders. Each of these is backed by a wall supporting climbers of many kinds, some of which would be scarcely hardy in less sheltered places.

Below the terraces is a large lawn along the edge of which are ten yews, clipped to the shape of chessmen, and four Irish yews. These stand beside a low stone wall overlooking the park laid out by Lancelot 'Capability' Brown in the eighteenth century.

The grounds surrounding the castle are remarkable for their trees. There is an avenue of well-grown limes, and another over a mile long consisting of Spanish Chestnuts (*Castanea sativa*). Here, too, can be found an Evergreen Oak (*Quercus ilex*) planted, according to legend, on the day in 1600 when building of the house was begun, fine specimens of the Blue Cedar (*Cedrus atlantica glauca*), Lawson's Cypress, an ancient Judas Tree (*Cercis siliquastrum*), its trunk now prostrate, and very large specimens of *Cotinus coggygria* the Wig Tree or Smoke Tree. Chilham also boasts one of the oldest mulberries in England, the parent of many growing in Virginia, USA, grown from pieces taken there by one of the Digges family, who became Governor of Virginia, and many other specimen trees.

Against the south wall of the castle is a wisteria, said to be the first to be planted in this country. This and a very large Banksian Rose, nearly 150 years old, completely cover the wall.

Chilham Castle, approached through Chilham village lies five miles south-west of Canterbury, just off the A252.

Overleaf: Flights of brick steps of unusual design connect the various terraces.

Below left: Herbaceous borders backed by brick walls line the terraces at Chilham Castle. Climbing plants are grown against the walls and behind them can be seen some of the topiary specimens. Below: Looking from the terraces over the topiary chessmen to the park beyond.

Cliveden

A wide and famous view of the River Thames flowing between steep, wooded slopes seen over an immense lawn lingers in the mind's eye after a visit to the famous house and gardens at Cliveden, Buckinghamshire. The diarist, John Evelyn, described it in 1679: . . .'tis a romantic object, and the place altogether answers the most poetical description that can be made . . . on the platform is a circular view to the utmost verge of the horizon, which with the serpenting of the Thames is admirably surprising.'

This view is enjoyed from the dominating architectural feature at Cliveden, the great red brick terrace built by William Winde in 1666. Upon it now stands a handsome Victorian building. An array of shrubs and climbers is trained against the terrace and at its base is a wide, well-planted border. The view is enhanced by grey Atlas Cedars flanking the lawn and box-edged parterres of original design. Beside the lawn a delightful path winds down to the riverside.

Elsewhere there is much worth seeing, including the eighteenth century temples by Giacomo Leoni, who helped to introduce the Palladian architectural movement in Britain. A Japanese-style garden surrounds a temple-like building surmounted by a weird, fish-like figure of a monster. The garden has matured Japanese Maples, bamboos and other shrubs. A wide, grass avenue has as its focal point a glistening white, ornate fountain. There is also a water garden with a good selection of water-lilies. The shrubberies are interesting.

Cliveden is two miles north of Taplow on th B476 road to Hedsor. The road forms the northern and eastern boundaries to the grounds, the entrance being at Feathers lodge on the east side.

Below: The south front and terrace of Cliveden, constructed in 1666, overlooking an old parterre, from which a wealth of tree planting is to be seen.

Right: The pagoda used in the Great Exhibition of 1851 makes a focal point in the Japanese Garden.

Below: Magnolia and cherry trees and the old Canning Oak in the spring. The Cliveden reach of the Thames can be seen beyond, as the estate enjoys a unique position on the high ground above the river.

Compton Acres

The story of this series of gardens began just after the 1914–18 War, when the late T. W. Simpson, who had built a house on the site, began to convert what was largely moorland overlooking Poole Harbour into gardens of different styles. He spent £220,000 in landscaping, importing stone and rock, garden ornaments and plants. During the Second World War, the gardens deteriorated badly but were restored by the next owner and opened to the public in 1952.

In 1964 the present owners, Mr and Mrs Brady, bought the estate and continued to open the gardens.

The Glen, Rock and Water Gardens contain a sub-tropical section with a chain of small lakes around which palms, mimosas, jacarandas, eucalyptus, bamboos and rhododendrons from the Himalayas grow. The path continues through a short tunnel to the rock garden. Here, rustic bridges cross the pools in which king carp swim among water lilies. From it can be seen the cascades which provide the water. Nearby is a viewpoint looking down the glen spread out below.

The Japanese Garden, surrounding an irregular pool, crossed by stepping stones, was built in the proper Japanese style, to the plans of a Japanese architect, using materials brought from Japan. Pagodas, carved lanterns, figures and gateways – all full of symbolic meaning – abound. The plants too, are Japanese. As a contrast there is the garden built in the Roman manner from which, past herbaceous borders, the Italian Garden is reached. It is a large canal-like pool, its surroundings highly formal and decorated with urns and statues.

Finally, there is the Palm Court with more valuable statuary and a Wishing Well into which the visitor may throw money for charity.

The gardens are in Canford Cliffs Road, midway between Bournemouth and Poole.

Left: The authentic statuary and some of the oriental planting to be seen at Crompton Acres' Japanese garden.

Right: The highly formal Italian Garden with its canal-like pool decorated with urns and statues.

Below: The Rock Garden crossed with rustic bridges. The pools are filled with water lillies around which King Carp swim.

Compton Wynyates

Lying hidden in a secluded Warwickshire valley, the house at Compton Wynyates is one of the most beautiful and picturesquely situated Tudor buildings in Britain. It has always belonged to the Compton family, and is the home of its present head, the 6th Marquess of Northampton. It was the birthplace in 1632 of Henry Compton, a most remarkable and forthright character who, when he became Bishop of London in 1675, made at Fulham Palace a most remarkable collection of trees and plants, many of them first introductions from eastern North America.

This glorious house has had a chequered career, having entertained royalty, been sacked by Cromwellians, been ordered to be pulled down by its owner to help pay his debts, but saved by a steward who ignored his instructions, and later rescued and restored.

Around it the ground is levelled below the now grassy remains of old terraces. The garden, of neither great size nor age, is rectangular. It is planted more or less regularly with evergreens clipped, however, most irregularly into a variety of shapes. Among them are grown herbaceous plants and roses, while a few standard trees give added variety. Thus a comparatively modern garden adds greatly to this historic house, and is seen to great effect when looked down upon from the grassy slopes that lead up to the surrounding woods.

Compton Wynyates is just north of the B4035 Banbury – Shipston road, ten miles west of Banbury.

The estate of Compton Wynyates lies in a valley on the Warwickshire border, and is seen at its best when looked down upon from the surrounding hills.
Below: The house in late spring with tulips adding bright colour to the dark evergreens.

Above: The remarkable Tudor house stands amid clipped evergreens neatly shaped into an assortment of formal and unrelated designs.

Right: In summer the herbaceous plants and roses, together with a few standard trees, add variety to the evergreens, originally planted to make the maintenance of the garden easier.

Cotehele

The route to Cotehele lies through winding Cornish lanes, emerging under ancient sycamores. There the squat, grey medieval tower of this ancient place rises from a cluster of granite buildings. Standing on a small plateau, with the River Tamar not far away below, it is possible to see the banks on the opposite side through the tops of the trees lower down a small valley.

Near the house are conventional flower beds set in the grass. On and around the old walls, in sheltered corners, are trees and shrubs. There is the silver wattle (*Acacia dealbata*) from the Australian continent, with silvery leaves and scented yellow flowers that open early in the year. The evergreen Macartney rose (*Rosa bracteata*) (so called because it was brought from China in 1793 by Lord Macartney) climbs up a wall – a giant in every way (including its thorns) bearing its large white single flowers over a long period.

A short tunnel leads into a garden planted with greater informality. At its head a pond is the principal feature: from it a stream overflows and tumbles down the valley. On the damp margins waterside plants such as primulas, irises and gunnera, with leaves that may be six feet across, are found. Here, too, is a remarkable building with a domed roof, which is a medieval dove-cot. The banks either side are planted in a typical Cornish manner with rhododendrons, azaleas, maples, bamboos and hardy palms.

Cotehele is a National Trust property. It is situated on the west bank of the River Tamar, two miles west of Calstock by footpath or six miles by road, and 14 miles from Plymouth via the Tamar Bridge. It can also be reached from Plymouth by water.

Below left: The old dovecote or columbarium with some of the many rhododendrons which are a feature of the garden.
Below: White wisteria shrouds this door in the wall.

Above: The ancient house, made of granite, its walls supporting many plants, and part of the terraced garden.

Right: The brilliant approach to the house in spring.

Crathes

The tall grey building with its fanciful tower, so typical of Scotland, rises among the wooded coppices above the River Dee. It has a venerable history of gardening, with lime tree walks and yew hedges dating back to the eighteenth century. The remarkable garden we now see, making splendid use of a romantic setting, is largely the work of Sir James Burnett of Leys.

The grounds are divided into a series of rectangles, some of which are framed with old yew hedges, where choice and unusual, and sometimes difficult, plants will thrive.

From the range of greenhouses runs the long path to the doocot, or dove-cot. The border beside it includes the California Laurel, *Umbellularia californica*, the Tibetan Cherry with bark like highly polished mahogany, and the large Tree Peony, *Paeonia delavayi*, with dark blood-red flowers.

The approaches to the castle and the avenues are of particular interest, planted as they are with magnificent old Scots Pine, Douglas Fir, the rare Japanese Lacquer Trees, Antarctic Beeches from South America and New Zealand, the true Chinese Cotton Tree, the weeping Brewer's Spruce, and a survivor from prehistoric time, the Dawn Redwood. Crathes Castle, a property of the National Trust for Scotland, lies in Grampian, a little north of the A93, about 14 miles west of the city of Aberdeen.

Below: A view of Crathes Castle tower from the garden with its lime tree walks and yew hedges dating back to the eighteenth century.

Above and above left: The grounds of Crathes Castle are divided into a series of rectangles that are more or less regular and are planted to provide an effective arrangement of colour throughout the year.

Right: The view of the castle across the wide sweeping lawn.

60

Dartington Hall

Dartington Hall was built in the fourteenth century by John Holland, Duke of Exeter, a jouster of international fame. The site of his tournament ground has now been turned into a lawn set against the ruins of old buildings. On it stands an effective line of Irish Yews, the 'Twelve Apostles', while around it are some very ancient Sweet Chestnuts and on the bank above (now a series of grass terraces, so making the old Tilt Yard into an open-air theatre) is a magnificent Monterey Pine. At the end of the terrace is a great flight of steps leading through a Heath Garden.

The rest of the garden, on an undulating slope, is largely designed around a number of magnificent old trees; beeches, London planes, cedars, tulip trees, holm and Lucombe oaks, and a giant turkey oak. Among them have been planted glades of newer trees and shrubs. By the Azalea Dell is a round pond in which two swans carved in granite stand on an old cider mill; elsewhere contemporary sculpture is most effectively placed, notably Henry Moore's 'Reclining Woman'.

Walking around the wide and winding grass paths, one finds magnolias, cherries and rhododendrons as well as an exceptionally large Handkerchief Tree. This fine modern garden in a setting of ancient buildings and trees was begun after the First World War and was designed by an American, Mrs Beatrix Farrand, with later additions by Mr P. S. Cane.

Dartington Hall lies about one mile out of Totnes, Devon on the A384 in the direction of Ashburton.

Overleaf: The house, some parts of which date back to the fourteenth century, can be seen in spring through the trees.

Far left: Standing on the far side of the Tilt yard, the line of Irish yews known as the 'Twelve Apostles'.
Left: A rhododendron path leads to the tower of a derelict church.

Left: A contemporary sculpture by Henry Moore is a twentieth century addition to the old garden.

East Lambrook

East Lambrook Manor in Somerset was the home of Margery Fish, the well-known gardening writer. The garden was made by Mrs Fish and her husband in 1937 round the fifteenth century house and is now preserved as a memorial to her. It is unique in that it has a true cottage atmosphere, with close and luxuriant planting.

Many rare and interesting plants are grown alongside old favourites, and the garden is a good example of natural gardening, which is popular today. Great use is made of the old walls, and foliage plays a big part in a scheme designed to be interesting at all seasons. A large variegated sycamore dominates the lawn at the back of the house, and the wide border under a high wall is always colourful. Clipped conifers and neat hedges contrast with the billowing silver foliage and branching euphorbias in the terraced garden beside the house.

There is a small silver garden facing south, and the old farm ditch, which originally separated two orchards, makes an unusual woodland garden. Here old primroses, hellebores and hardy geraniums grow under pollarded willows, while exotic plants, ornamental grasses and green flowers are cultivated in another small garden.

East Lambrook is three miles north of A303, between Ilchester and Ilminster. It is nine miles from Yeovil and 18 from Taunton.

Left: East Lambrook Manor is a sophisticated cottage garden, where first-class varieties of plants, both old-fashioned and modern, are planted closely together in a seeming confusion, yet their growth is carefully controlled.

*Right: Clipped conifers form a
miniature avenue with plants
sprawled along the pathway.*

*Below: A large variegated sycamore
dominates the lawn.*
*Below right: Close and luxuriant
planting are a major feature of this
garden and helps add to the friendly
cottage atmosphere.*

Glendurgan

This famous Cornish garden, now the property of the National Trust, gets its name from the lovely glen which it occupies. This curls downwards from the high ground on which the house stands to the tiny hamlet of Durgan on the northern side of the Helford River. It is a spot of great natural beauty, sufficiently sheltered and mild to permit the cultivation of many exotic trees and shrubs which grow here as freely as in their native countries.

On the upper lawn, near the house, the visitor is greeted by the great succulent rosettes of a Mexican Agave and in the valley below the South American evergreen, *Drimys winteri*, is planted in groves and has grown to tree-like proportions. Rhododendrons and azaleas of many kinds thrive in this valley including a large number of the more tender varieties some of which have richly fragrant flowers. On the damper ground Asiatic primulas have naturalised themselves and grow as freely as native primroses.

But in addition to its rare and beautiful plants, Glendurgan possesses an unusual interest in a garden of this type. On the steepest part of the slope below the house is a large maze formed of close-clipped laurel with a whitebeam as its centre-piece. When viewed from a distance at the far side of the valley it appears as a complex pattern and it also makes an unexpectedly formal feature in this relatively wild section of the garden.

Near the house is a large walled garden, no doubt formerly used for fruit and vegetables but now planted with flowers including many climbing plants. From this point a path leads along the top of the valley to a fine viewpoint over the river estuary.

Glendurgan is four miles south west of Falmouth, on the road to Helford Passage.

Above: The mild, sheltered climate of Glendurgan allows many exotic species to be cultivated. Here, the lawn above the valley with a fine specimen of Agave americana.
Left: The house with clumps of rhododendrons and azaleas some of the many kinds that thrive here.

Right: One of the few formal features at Glendurgan, the Laurel maze seen from the far side of the valley. The centre point is formed by a whitebeam.

Below: In May, the grassy slopes are thick with bluebells.
Below right: In the damp atmosphere by the river, primulas (many introductions) and gunneras flourish.

Haddon Hall

The castle-like building of Haddon Hall sprawls over the end of a Derbyshire hillside with the River Wye curling below. The house itself acts as a backdrop for many climbing plants and a short flight of steps from the exquisite long gallery leads into a small, rectangular garden cut into geometrically-shaped flower beds.

This is the beginning of a very broad terrace with, on the right, a beautiful seventeenth century carved stone balustrade. To the left are hedges and minor terraces below the tree-clad rising slopes. To the right is a view down the long and beautiful south front of the house. The ground slopes steeply and interestingly in two directions, first along the side of the building and then, away from that, even more steeply to the river below. There is a wonderful view down on a series of small terrace-like gardens at different levels, linked by flights of steps and supported by walls.

The first flight is elegant and stylish, like the balustrade, and leads to a large rectangular lawn with a fountain at its centre. Great use of roses is made in this upper part of the garden. Below this the retaining walls are striking in their contrast. Upon them many plants are naturalised, others are trained against them, while interesting plants are grown in the beds at their base.

Haddon Hall is two miles south-east of Bakewell and six and a half miles north of Matlock on the A6 Buxton to Matlock road.

Left: The terraces at Haddon Hall are connected by this fine stone stairway, itself used as a support for many fine specimens of trailing plants.

Above: Full use is made of the walls of the house. These shelter and support a wide variety of climbers and other shrubs which help to provide colour and interest against the grey stone.

*Above: The broad lawn is
surrounded by rose beds.
Above right: A glimpse of the
balustraded parapet to the top of the
terrace.*

*Right: A vigorous clematis grows
over an old mullioned window.*

Hampton Court

The garden of this palace was the first in Britain to be made in the magnificent style of the Renaissance. First laid out in 1514, with sheltered alley-ways, and elaborate knots and fountains, the jealous Henry VIII acquired it from Cardinal Wolsey in 1529 and greatly enlarged and elaborated upon the original design. He had a magnificent mount, or viewpoint, constructed on a foundation of a quarter of a million bricks and surmounted it by a magnificent arbour. New flower beds surrounded by painted rails were laid out and effigies of heraldic beasts were erected. Unfortunately, none of this remains today, but pictures of it are on display in the Palace. To give an idea of what the original garden was like, a small knot garden was planted in 1924 and the initials E.R. with the date 1568 were carved on the bay window overlooking it.

Far more remains of the next phase of the garden which was designed by London and Wise for William III and Mary at the time of Wren's additions to the Palace. This is the great Fountain Garden with its avenues radiating from the magnificent portico at the centre of the east front. It is now greatly changed – there were originally several more fountains and in what is now grass was an intricate network of flower beds, or parterre.

Below: Henry VIII's Pond or Sunken Garden at Hampton Court is planted up each spring and autumn to ensure a continuous display of colour.

Above: Much of the original formal French design of Hampton Court remains, including the Canal or 'Long Water'.
Above right: A view across Henry VIII's Pond or Sunken Garden looking across to the Banqueting House.

Right: The seventeenth-century garden was replanned and restored in period style.

Another relic of this period is the maze near the lion gate. This was at one corner of an area of trees and shrubs intersected by paths winding in and out, called The Wilderness. Nearby is the tilt yard, the scene of tournaments in the time of Henry VIII, which has now been turned into a modern garden.

To the south of Wren's building lies the large Privy Garden laid out formally with paths, lawns and trees and decorated with statuary and a fountain. This, too, was much more ornate with scroll-like flower beds in the days of William and Mary. On either side the ground is raised. That on the west is an alleyway of wych elms called Queen Mary's Bower. By the foot of the steps leading to it is a gateway passing a series of small flower gardens enclosed within brick walls known as the Tudor Garden.

Hampton Court Palace lies on the North bank of the Thames not far from Kingston. It is easily reached by rail from Waterloo or by Green Line bus. It is well signposted and motorists can approach it by turning off the A3 at the Scilly Isles roundabout near Esher, or by crossing Kingston Bridge and turning left.

Harewood House

The magnificent estate of Harewood near Leeds, Yorkshire, provides outstanding examples of two entirely distinct types of garden, both typical of their period. One is a fine example of the English informal landscape of the late eighteenth century, the other is laid out on the lines of mid-Victorian formality.

In the 1840s, the then Countess of Harewood engaged Sir Charles Barry (who later laid out, in a similar style, the gardens at Shrubland, Suffolk, and Trentham, Staffordshire) to design the formal garden. The present ornate garden front in an Italian manner is linked to the landscape by means of terraces in the same florid, yet undeniably grand manner. A large fountain plays on the main level, while statuary and the vases placed around it form decoratively formal beds, colourfully planted according to the season.

The lake designed by 'Capability' Brown, visible some way off over grass and backed by banks of trees (badly damaged some years ago by a gale, but now replanted) helps to make one of his best scenic efforts. It is a delightful walk down to it, winding among old trees. Near one end of the lake a 'pleasure garden' contains a charming summer house 'guarded' by two stone owls.

Harewood lies on the A61 Leeds-Harrogate Road, eight miles north of Leeds and seven south of Harrogate.

Below left: In front of the house is a colourful formal garden designed by Sir Charles Barry. The Victorian style contrasts with the surrounding informal garden.
Below: The delightful walk beside the lake, designed by 'Capability' Brown.
Bottom: A cascade runs alongside the path which leads to the lake and is planted with the colourful azaleas.

Right: The formal garden at Harewood laid out by Sir Charles Barry, seen from the air.

Below: The Rose Garden provides a splendid colour at the edge of the lake.

Harlow Car

Not far from the centre of Harrogate, on a site of 40 acres, there has been formed, since 1948, a remarkable garden, finely landscaped and interestingly planted, the purpose of which is to demonstrate what plants and what types of gardening are possible in the bleak conditions of the north. Here, the Northern Horticultural Society is doing for its particular locality what the Royal Horticultural Society does at Wisley.

From the distinguished entrance gate, a long, wide grass 'broad walk' is bordered with shrubs and herbaceous plants. Behind those on the left are a very successful heath garden, well suited to the district, and a rock garden. Behind the beds on the right, at the top, are the glasshouses, rose beds, and a trials area.

At the bottom of this walk is a stream, crossed at the point where there is a water garden. The opposite bank slopes up and is mostly wooded, with a glimpse of a portico of Doric columns (from the old facade of Harrogate's Spa Rooms). The woodland, extending a considerable distance on either side, is under-planted with many shrubs, and further away to the right there is a promising young arboretum.

These are but the principal features of a place of great practical interest to all northern gardeners and of delight to all throughout the year.

The gardens are situated in Crag Lane, a turning off the B6162, about a mile and a half from the centre of Harrogate, on the Otley Road.

Above: The naturalized daffodils in light woodland.

Left: The gardens of the Northern Horticultural Society at Harlow Car attract thousands of visitors each year and show exactly what can be achieved in the colder conditions of the north of England. The rhododendrons and azaleas are surprisingly successful.
Overleaf: The Rose Garden.

Hidcote

Hidcote lies on the scarp of the Cotswolds between Stratford-on-Avon and Broadway with the Avon Vale spread out below.

The garden, which extends to about ten acres, is entirely the creation of an American, the late Major Lawrence Johnston, who acquired the place at the beginning of this century. It was a small bleak farmhouse with a solitary cedar in front of it and a clump of beech trees some yards away. On this unpromising site, using hedges for protection, Major Johnston made this garden which is now mature. Leading from the cedar there is a straight central alleyway passing through a series of small compartment-like gardens, each one treated differently; one for example contains red foliaged and red-flowered plants, another an alleyway which passes between twin gazebos and continues between hornbeams on trunks, the foliage closely clipped in the French manner; this is the Stilt Garden. In Mrs Winthrop's Garden, named after Major Johnston's mother, yellow predominates. A raised circular pool almost fills another small 'compartment'. The last compartment ends in a fine old gateway, through which is unexpectedly revealed a wide view over Shakespeare's country. In some of the tall, well-kept hedges several kinds of plants are used giving them a variegated appearance. These are often referred to as 'tapestry' hedges. In the Fuchsia Garden, yew, box, holly, beech and hornbeam are used in the hedges, giving different textures and colours.

Below: The design at Hidcote is very much designed on compartments and as such it makes an ideal place to inspire the visitor with a garden of his own. Looking along the double mixed borders to the Cedar of Lebanon, dark-foliaged plants contrast with the roses.

Above: The Bathing Pool Garden surrounded by tall hedges, with topiary birds in the background.
Above right: Part of the Pillar Garden dominated by topiary columns in clipped yew.

Right: Part of the double mixed border leading to the twin garden houses or gazebos, of which one is shown.

There is a certain amount of topiary, mainly birds, but tall columns of yew dominate the Pillar Garden.

The other main feature is a wild garden. This follows a stream that meanders down the hill, along whose sides are planted many fine trees, flowering shrubs and moisture-loving plants to make a feature as informal as the compartment gardens are formal. These two axes are linked by further small gardens.

Elsewhere there are collections of old and species roses and clematis and a wide lawn sweeping up to the old beech tree. Throughout the garden there are fine examples of planting and good specimens of unusual plants.

The garden is now owned by the National Trust. It is at Hidcote Bartrim, three miles NE of Chipping Campden, one mile E of the A46 and of the B4081.

Kew Gardens

The Royal Botanic Gardens, Kew, Surrey, covering an area of 300 acres on the south side of the River Thames, are the home of one of the most extensive collections of plants in the world. A garden for a botanical collection was started over 200 years ago by Princess Augusta, widow of the Prince of Wales who, with the help of John Stuart, the Earl of Bute, began the garden in the grounds of her home at Kew House. The garden of neighbouring Richmond House was later linked with Kew House garden, and the whole property taken over by the nation in 1841.

Sir William Chambers (1723-96), the British architect, designed a fine orangery and was also responsible for the fantastic pagoda built in the Chinese style.

There is interest all the year round at Kew, and even in winter, or on a day of unpleasant weather, it is well worth visiting the fernery and conservatory and cactus, orchid and alpine houses near the main gate. The famous rock garden is also in this part of the gardens. Near the Victorian Gate stands the 120-year old palm house, the most beautiful building incorporating glass in its construction in Britain. In spring the Rhododendron dell and nearby Azalea and Magnolia gardens are most delightful, with a fine view across the river to Syon House, seat of the Duke of Northumberland.

From this part of the garden an avenue of oaks leads to the palm house and lake, and from the pagoda you can reach the large temperate house, and the greenhouse containing a collection of Australian plants. These are some of the main features, but everywhere there is something of beauty or interest for the visitor, not excepting the new historical garden by Kew Palace.

Kew Gardens are one mile from Richmond and approached from London by bus, Underground service, or, in summer, by boat.

Below left: The temperate house at Kew which contains a remarkable and large collection of plants.
Below: The Chinese-style pagoda, designed by Sir William Chambers in the eighteenth century, is one of the more famous and eccentric features of Kew Gardens.

Above: An oriental temple seen in a perfect setting among azaleas.

Right: The Palm House at Kew, designed by Decimus Burton, one of the most beautiful buildings incorporating glass in Britain.

Killerton Park

Killerton Park is first visible as a hill which, even from a distance, is clearly seen to be planted with trees that are not usually seen in the English landscape. The hill is of acid volcanic soil in which rhododendrons and other lime-haters thrive. The climate is mild and border-line trees such as eucalyptus grow quite happily.

The Aclands have lived in the district since the early fifteenth century. It was Sir Thomas Acland, the tenth baronet, who, well aware of the excellence of his site and the fact that he could grow tender plants, began the garden just after the Napoleonic wars. He engaged a local nurseryman, Robert Veitch, a Scot. Veitch later moved to Exeter and the family firm that he established was, until the beginning of the present century, the outstanding introducer of plants from America and China.

Entering the grounds above the house (which is not open to the public), one is led below the hill, passing some exceptionally fine specimens of trees and rhododendrons scattered among the grass. Then the climb begins, passing a Victorian rustic summerhouse, called the 'Bear House' because a bear was once kept in it. The floor is laid with the knucklebones of deer. Above it is an old rock-garden below which is an Ice House dating from the mid-nineteenth century. Up on the hill, with its wide views to Dartmoor, there are several paths. There is a walk by great beech trees, below which are large cork oaks. High up, there is a rhododendron glade and on the edge of the grounds a band of azaleas in blazing colours. In spring, there are masses of daffodils. Following the guide, exceptional specimens of magnolia, many rare conifers, the flaming embothrium from South America and eucalyptus from the Australian continent may be seen.

In this mild climate there is much to be seen very early in the year, and thence onward throughout the seasons. Autumn is a particularly pleasant time to see the gardens, as the leaves of many of the trees colour beautifully before they fall.

Killerton Park, a National Trust property, is reached by a minor road (B3185) branching off to the left, seven miles north of Exeter on A38.

Left: The mild climate of Devonshire encourages luxuriant growth and tender plants to flourish at Killerton Park.

*Right: In spring the natural
planting of daffodils and the vista
over the distant hills, extends the
natural beauty of Killerton.*

*Below: Annuals add colour and a
sense of profusion to the garden in
summer.*

Knightshayes

Knightshayes Court stands on a hillside overlooking the lovely valley of the River Exe. It is a site perfectly made for gardening, and successive generations have made good use of it for at least a hundred years. An avenue of large trees which sweeps up from the entrance gate encloses the drive to the house. The broad terrace accommodating the house was no doubt cut out of the hillside in Victorian times and the series of intimate gardens enclosed in thick yew hedges.

But it is during the last forty years that Knightshayes Court has acquired international fame for its rich and growing collection of exotic plants arranged with the utmost skill by Sir John and Lady Heathcote Amory. The slopes below the house have been enriched with fine trees, rhododendrons and other shrubs; a large scree bed below the formal gardens provides ideal conditions for gentians and choice alpine plants and the terrace itself has been richly planted, though one of the enclosed gardens remains, for contrast, almost completely unplanted, with only a circular pool and one white marble statue as ornament.

The main woodland garden, still in process of enlargement, lies beyond, laid out in long curving beds, built up where necessary with peat blocks and containing a vast collection of plants, including the tiny ones so often neglected in gardens of this magnitude. Among the rhododendrons, azaleas, pieris, magnolias, daphnes, and other shrubs are Dog's Tooth violets, wood-lilies, hellebores, hostas, dicentras, violets and many more.

To the west of the house a deep dell containing a pool has been surrounded by deciduous azaleas, underplanted with bluebells, a magnificent spectacle in spring.

Knightshayes lies one and a half miles north-east of Tiverton in Devon. Bus services run from Tiverton to Taunton and Minehead, and from Exeter to Minehead: alight at Bolham. The house, gardens and grounds are now managed by the National Trust.

Below left: The formal garden set below the house contrasts well with the woodland planting.
Below: A stone seat set amongst well-trimmed hedges in the formal garden.

Above: Part of the profusion of plants that make up the Woodland Garden in Spring.

Right: A series of intimate gardens enclosed by clipped yew hedges surround the house. This is a corner of the rock garden.

Lanhydrock

Unlike most Cornish gardens, Lanhydrock is not situated close to the coast, but well inland overlooking the richly wooded valley of the River Fowey. A plan shows that there was a good garden here in 1694, but the present gardens were laid out from the mid-nineteenth century onwards with considerable alterations and additions in the nineteen-thirties.

The house is reached by a long avenue of sycamores planted in 1648, and is guarded by the highly decorated seventeenth-century Gatehouse. Around this, and in front of the house itself, the gardens are formal. Neat pyramids of Irish yews arise with regularity, and tidy beds of tulips and forget-me-nots, followed later by roses, are within clipped hedges which in turn are guarded from the outside world by Victorian granite walls decorated with finials. Here will be found exceptionally fine urns modelled by Louis Ballin, Goldsmith to Louis XIV of France. Against the house itself are good specimens of the evergreen, late-flowering *Magnolia grandiflora*, a native of the south-eastern states of the USA.

Behind and above the house is the Higher Garden which contains twentieth century plantings of trees and shrubs among older specimens and through them delightful views are obtained of the house and gardens below.

There is always something to see. In early spring there are the giant-flowered *Magnolia cambellii* and *M. mollicomata*. A great variety of Himalayan and Chinese rhododendrons bloom into June, when the astonishing Japanese Dogwood (*Cornus kousa*) is a remarkable sight. Later in the season, hydrangeas are followed by rich autumn leaf-colour. At all times, fine exotic conifers, and particularly some majestic Irish yews, impart a sense of dignity.

Lanhydrock, a property of the National Trust, is two and a half miles south of Bodmin; from the A38 turn south at Carminow Cross; from Bodmin or Lostwithiel take the B3268. Bus 54 (Lostwithiel, Bodmin, Wadebridge) stops at the gate.

Below: The seventeenth century Gatehouse, the wall with its nineteenth century finials and the house set against the background of the woodland garden.

Above: One of the bronze urns, said to be the work of Louis Ballin, goldsmith to Louis XIV, surrounded by formal rose beds.

Above right: The seventeenth century gatehouse looking inwards towards the formal garden.

Right: Part of the formal garden around the house.

Montacute House

Montacute House was finished near the end of Queen Elizabeth I's reign. It is the most splendid and complete example of its kind remaining to us. The present garden bears little resemblance to the original for one reason: the present entrance side of the house was originally the back.

Near the entrance it is worth noticing two interesting trees. Both are specimens of the Monterey cypress (*Cupressus macrocarpa*); one has been kept clipped as a piece of topiary, while the other has grown into a giant, probably the biggest specimen in Britain.

Against the north end of the house is a sunken lawn garden, bordered with formal evergreens, and at its centre a fountain. Designed by R. S. Balfour in 1894, its simple lines are very effective when looked down upon from the windows above. The balustrading and the obelisk finials surmounting it so exactly match the similar features on the older walls that, with the passage of time, it is difficult to realise that they were made nearly three centuries later. By the south corner of the house, we ascend a broad flight of steps into a courtyard lying against the long and magnificent east front. At its corners are two exquisite pavilions, while the surrounding walls carry ornaments typical of the Elizabethan age, including two gazebos. There is no comparable piece of garden architecture still in existence.

Below: The elegant Elizabethan Montacute House, one of the most complete examples of this period remaining. However, there is one major difference – the original entrance of the house is now the back.

Above: The northern sunken lawn garden has a formal lily pool and fountain.
Above right: A pavilion overlooking the Courtyard Garden on the east side of the house.

Right: The Conservatory at the end of the terrace now houses ferns.

Now grassed over apart from a broad walk around it, and the walls most beautifully planted, the place is a gem, although it was originally the entrance court for the arrival and departure of carriages, rather than a garden.

Passing from it to the south side of the house, we find enclosed gardens, some of the yews in which are of considerable age.

A charming small nineteenth century conservatory built in a Tudor style stands near the north corner. In the Long Gallery there is now on permanent loan from the National Portrait Gallery, a magnificent exhibition of one hundred Elizabethan and Jacobean portraits. The house and gallery have been also recently decorated.

Montacute, a National Trust property, is four miles west of Yeovil, on the north side of A3088. Note that dogs and pushchairs are not allowed in the house or gardens, but the gardens are accessible to visitors in wheelchairs.

Mount Stewart

Mount Stewart is one of the last British gardens to be laid out in the grand manner. Although it already looks mature, the planning and planting of its 78 acres were not begun by its creator, the 7th Marchioness of Londonderry, until 1921.

Almost an island, lying between two loughs and subject to the mild airs of the Gulf Stream, this garden boasts a wide range of plants that would elsewhere be tender. Making use of the visual beauties of the scenery, formality and informality are combined in a series of gardens surrounded by woodland and inter-woven with paths, lavishly planted with rhododendrons, camellias, eucalyptuses, magnolias and a selection of other rarities.

Only some of the gardens can be described here. That on the south side of the house, and running its length, is formal and in the Italian manner, having as its main inspiration the villas Gamberaia and Caprarola, but employing planting material that was unknown in the days when these famous Italian gardens were made, the parterres containing both rare shrubs and herbaceous plants. The garden along the west side of the house, with a pergola, is otherwise sunk and enclosed by macrocarpa hedges.

To the north lie the woodland and waterside walks, with at one point an outcrop of rock around which was made a natural rock garden.

Another interesting feature, of particularly national interest, is the Shramrock Garden. It is paved, and the plan is that of a Shamrock. At its centre is a bed, the shape of the Red Hand of Ulster planted with the red-foliaged *Iresine herbstii*. The surrounding hedge carries a hunting scene in topiary work.

Mount Stewart is a National Trust property. It lies on the eastern shore of Strangford Lough, five miles south-east of Newtownards, 15 miles east of Belfast on the north side of the Belfast-Portaferry road (A20).

Left: The gardens at Mount Stewart consist of a series of gardens, some formal and others informal, skilfully created by Lady Londonderry after the First World War. The Tin-N'An Oge or Burial Ground is set out in a formal manner with paved paths and a small formal water garden at the centre.

Above: The Spanish Garden set out in formal manner is a sunken garden. Here the formal pool lies below an impressive flight of steps which leads down from the southern facade of the house, bordered by a massive hedge.

Right: Another view of the Spanish Garden, in spring, where naturalised planting marries the formal and natural styles.

Nymans

The gardens at Nymans, Sussex, are best described as a blend of formal and informal in which the trees, shrubs and plants – always of fine quality – and their arrangement play a predominant part. The garden, on well-drained, fertile sandy loam was begun by Mr Ludwig Messel eighty years ago. His friends, the famous gardeners William Robinson and Gertrude Jekyll advised and encouraged him on its development. It is a garden today with a surprising feature: the house which it surrounded is largely a burned-out shell – a true ruin of grey stone, rather than those of the artificial kind such as the follies of the eighteenth century. Strangely, the fire did little damage to the tender plants that were sheltered by the walls of the building; they now ramble inside the glass windows.

Around the house on one side are the lawns, with banks of flowering shrubs, and on the other, a walled garden with an Italian fountain at its centre, with topiary around it. A heather garden, one of the first in the country, a rose garden and a pinetum are among the other pleasant parts of the garden, in which originated that fine shrub, *Eucryphia* 'Nymansay'. This last, indeed, with its large white flowers, with golden centres in late summer, is freely planted among the sombre conifers in the pinetum. In an area curiously called a reserve garden, under Scots pines, the Chinese rhododendrons such as the huge-leaved *R. sinogrande* flourish. Past them a glade is designed to display the autumn colours of foliage and berries – enkianthus, pyracantha, *Rosa moyesii* and the Chinese Maples. Here, too, is the dense carpet of spring-flowering dwarf rhododendrons from the mountains of western China. Beyond is an area of exceptional interest called Tasmania, in which grow plants from that country and the Andes.

The gardens, now in the care of the National Trust, lie on the B2114, a little way off the A23 (London–Brighton road), one mile south of the village of Handcross, five miles south of Crawley.

The foundations of the garden at Nymans were laid in 1885 by Ludwig Messel in collaboration with some of the best gardeners of the day, such as William Robinson and Gertrude Jekyll. Today, Nymans is famous for its rhododendrons and camellias.

Right: The house at Nymans, now a National Trust property, is little more than a ruin.

Below: The stone used to construct the grey calcined walls of the house and features such as the dovecote, shown here, has weathered attractively and blends with the trees and shrubs for which Nymans is famous.

Packwood House

Packwood House is a timber Tudor building with later additions. It stands in typical Warwickshire countryside among fields, enclosed by hedges, interspersed with copses.

The garden is within a series of walled enclosures laid out in beds beautifully and gaily planted with modern plants. There is also a small, formal water garden made in the present century. These alone would make Packwood a delightful place to visit. But there is more to see of exceptional interest. There is, for instance, a long wall ending in what looks to be an unusual eighteenth century gazebo. On examination, it proves to be nothing of the sort, but a small furnace house, whose purpose was to circulate hot fumes through flues within the wall, so warming it to prevent the frosting of fruit trees such as the peaches and nectarines that were once trained against it.

Another old wall across the garden has a fine gate. On passing through it and descending a semi-circular flight of steps, one sees a series of alcoves with arched

Left: One of the main features of Packwood House is the topiary garden. Made around 1650, tradition has it that it represents the Sermon on the Mount.

Below: Spring bedding flanks the long path.

Above: The fine wrought iron gate. The series of alcoves in the wall were once used to house bee hives or skeps when they were made of perishable straw.

tops on either side. These were made to shelter the old beehives, or skeps, when they were made of perishable straw.

Even more remarkable is the walk among large, neatly clipped yews, leading to an old 'mound', a raised mound of earth whose yew-crowned top is reached by a narrow, spiralling path. There is a tradition that this group of topiary represents the Sermon on the Mount.

Packwood House, a National Trust property, is reached by taking B4439 off A34 in the village of Hockley Heath, then after one and a half miles taking a minor road to the left; this passes between the buildings (identified by a sundial on one wall).

Penshurst Place

Penshurst Place, the birthplace of Sir Philip Sidney in 1554, is a venerable building erected over a period of nearly three hundred years starting in the early thirteenth century. In front and to one side of it the garden matches it admirably, and also has an air of antiquity, though it is mostly little more than one hundred years old. It is an example of clever reconstruction of a sixteenth or seventeenth century garden, which gives the building a dignified setting.

In front of the house is a large, rectangular parterre with raised terraces on two sides. The parterre beds are large and of simple design, some outlined in box and filled with red roses. Other beds are entirely planted with box cut into low moulded slabs. A large circular basin for water-lilies, with a central bronze statue of a youth, completes the design.

A yew-enclosed alley cuts across the garden, and there are also orchards, a

Left: An alley enclosed by yew hedges and topiary.

Below left: Prunus pissardii grown as standards in the cottage garden. Below: A glimpse through the yew hedges.

Above: Looking towards the eastern wall of the garden at Penshurst Place. The garden walls date from the reign of Elizabeth I.

Right: The large rectangular parterre with raised terraces at each side from which the design can be looked down upon.

typical feature of the Kent countryside. At one point the yew alley opens out into a large rectangle almost entirely filled by a pool enclosed by low, brick walls.

The entrance drive, at right angles to the yew alley, passes between wide herbaceous borders which are backed by apple trees, and between the drive and the great parterre are little orchard gardens each enclosed in yew. It is the free use of fruit trees in a formal setting that makes the garden so unique and gives it a Kentish flavour.

Penshurst Place is in Penshurst village on the B2176 road, three miles from the A26 road from Sevenoaks.

Polesden Lacey

This Regency house stands on a chalk ridge with wide views over undulating, park-like Surrey countryside and is surrounded by wide lawns and groups of trees. Its oldest and most distinguished feature is a terraced walk backed by aged trees and a view towards Ranmore Common. This walk was greatly extended by the dramatist R. B. Sheridan and bears his name.

Around the house the more or less formal lay-out is typical of the early decades of this century, consisting of a number of distinct but connected areas forming an extension to the house. One is a Rose Garden within old brick and flint walls, against which climbers are trained. Other small gardens are surrounded by clipped yew or box hedges.

Below these is a bank descending to the extensive lawn. On this sharp slope are many shrubs, including a remarkable mass of the low, spreading Knap Hill or Pfitzer Juniper (*Juniperus media pfitzeriana*). There are many fine trees on the lawn, including some tall, slender, Grey spruces (*Picea pungens glauca*), and notable beeches.

Polesden Lacey is a National Trust property. It is two and a half miles south of Bookham station and three miles west of Dorking. It is reached from A426 by a road running south from Great Bookham. The grounds also contain an open air theatre where Shakespearian plays are performed in June and July.

Left: On an estate famous for its trees, it is refreshing to find the cottage garden atmosphere among these roses.

Above: The Regency house, now the property of the National Trust, stands on high ground and commands wide views over the surrounding Surrey hills.

Right: A formal paved path with a rose pergola is guarded by heraldic beasts at the wrought iron gate.

Rowallane

The house and garden at Rowallane, Northern Ireland, lie not far from the sea in gently undulating country with beech and pine woods. The rainfall is typical of County Down, where they assure you it rains most days but seldom for long. Plants that like high humidity and dislike summer droughts thrive. Surrounding trees give good protection from gales and the soil is acid.

Driving up the long entrance drive shows that here is a garden full of good trees and shrubs. The late Hugh Armytage-Moore, who had a flair for design and the effective placing of his plants, began making the garden in 1903. He was a clever propagator and seed raiser just when there was a flood of new arrivals from western China, sent by E. H. Wilson, George Forrest and other successful collectors. The visitor can enjoy many mature specimens of these new introductions. Near the house are two gardens enclosed by high walls, against which are trained some rather tender shrubs, such as azara and tricuspidaria.

Leaving the formal gardens, you follow wandering paths in a series of distinctive areas each enclosed by low stone walls. The Spring Garden is full of azaleas and rhododendrons – both old and new kinds – making a brilliant display, with other trees and shrubs giving an equally rich autumn colour. The Old Wood is interspersed by great outcropping slabs of rock and Scots pines, and a small stream provides moisture for many of the smaller rhododendrons, rodgersias and lysichitums. Everywhere there is a feeling of space, and a sense of surprise on seeing little-known plants – always of great garden merit and placed with great skill. There are also many fine specimens of uncommon trees, including nothofagus, species of prunus and malus, abies and picea.

Rowallane is a National Trust property, 11 miles south-east of Belfast and one mile south of Saintfield village west of the A7 road to Downpatrick.

Below left: The natural outcrop of rocks at Rowallane provides a setting for a rock garden in which many unusual plants are to be found.

Below: In spring, the garden is at the height of its attractiveness with its collection of rhododendrons, azaleas and spring flowering shrubs.

Right: The name Rowallane is derived from a Celtic word meaning outcrop of rock, and this garden near Belfast has been made in such a location. The careful planting assures colour interest throughout the season.

Below: The artistry in the planting and the selection of plants at Rowallane was the hand of the later Hugh Armytage-Moor, a successful raiser of plants.

Rudding Park

The Regency house at Rudding Park, Yorkshire, simple in design and beautifully proportioned, stands in a slightly elevated situation overlooking a calm and restrained landscape. In the foreground are aged trees in a park which has been skilfully placed against a woodland background, one of Humphry Repton's finest landscapes. The level and spacious view is an integral part of the design. The effect of flat trim lawns surrounding the house is relieved by fine old trees, some now of unusual form, and by charming vases and other garden ornaments.

As was usual at the time when such gardens were designed, the flower garden was concealed in a walled enclosure away from the views. Today, between it and the house, a transformation has been effected. Among the trees a woodland garden, with glades and grassy walks and ornaments has been created with great skill and taste. Masses of primulas and intensely blue poppies flower underneath the shrubs, which are a surprising selection – kinds one expects only in the moist, mild countries of the South West. The large-leaved Chinese species of rhododendron and similar plants which grow so heartily, are also difficult to cultivate so far north.

Rudding Park is a short distance down a right turning off the A661 road three miles from Harrogate on the way to Wetherby.

Below left: A marble urn stands in a grassy clearing where four pathways meet.
Below: Double herbaceous borders, colourful for many weeks in summer, lead to the orangery.

Right: Blue flowered plants add colour to this woodland glade after the rhododendrons have finished flowering.

Below: A double border of roses underplanted with Alchemilla mollis and other plants.

Scotney

Nature and art combine in a scene of romantic beauty at Scotney Castle, Kent. The old castle dates from the fourteenth century, with later additions. Castle and moat, mellowed by time, are matched by the mature planted trees and carefully cultivated shrubs.

The medieval remains are concealed from the arriving visitor by the more modern front entrance to the house which was built to the design of Anthony Salvin in 1837. From the terrace of the house you can see below the castle and gardens with fields and woodlands rising beyond. The approach is made all the more dramatic by a path leading down along the lip of a quarry.

The combined effect of the garden and ruins is the result of careful design and skilful planting over many years. A great deal of work was done by the aunt and uncle of the late owner, Christopher Hussey, Esq, who continued their efforts with great care and thought. There are masses of fine shrubs, such as the older hybrid rhododendrons and azaleas, now of great size. Other shrubs include kalmias and leucothoës, which were features of the typical 'American' gardens fashionable in the last century. The shrubs are offset by undulating lawns and mature specimens of such conifers as Lawson's Cypress, the Redwood and Incense Cedar, which rise majestically over the scene. A contrast is the remarkably large, spreading example of the so-called Dwarf Spruce, *Picea abies* 'Clanbrassiliana', owing its name to the first Lord Clanbrassil, who introduced it from Ireland in about 1836. There are more recent plantings of roses, perennial flowers and shrubs, and also an old ice-house, formerly used for storage.

Scotney Castle is one mile south-east of Lamberhurst on the A21 road.

Overleaf: The combined effect of the garden and the ruins at Scotney is the striking result of careful planting over many years.

Below left: The combined setting of the old castle and the more modern house, reflected in the moat.
Below: Fine shrubs and rhododendrons in particular are massed together in a woodland garden. Their profusion is offset by smooth undulating lawns.

Sheffield Park

Unlike most gardens (Westonbirt Arboretum is another) Sheffield Park was designed with the knowledge that we often have glorious days in October and that by planting many trees and shrubs, comparatively recently introduced, the brilliance of autumn colour of thrilling intensity can extend the gardener's pleasures far into the autumn. In spring, the ground sheeted with bluebells, the gardens are equally enjoyable.

The garden as we now see it was the work of A. G. Soames. It was begun in 1909. His site was a series of five lakes in a descending chain, a 'Capability' Brown landscape with which Humphry Repton had been concerned. Around them Soames planted, usually in large numbers, trees and shrubs, often used only as single specimens, to give a series of carefully composed pictures and colour-schemes. Sometimes these are pale, the colours provided by giant bushes of rhododendrons, the Angelo hybrids, raised by Soames himself.

These are followed by the heavily-scented, large-flowered white and pink Loderi rhododendrons, raised at Leonardslee. At a later season the blue of massed gentians is a famous sight. The full glory of blazing colour is left for autumn, when among the rich greens of spiring conifers – a number of them rare – every shade of crimson, red, gold and yellow, particularly from massed plantings of the North American Tupelo tree, (*Nyssa sylvatica*) is reflected in the lakes.

Sheffield Park Gardens lie midway between East Grinstead and Lewes, east of A275, five miles north-west of Uckfield.

Below: Rhododendrons, water-side irises and trees grown for their colourful foliage contrast with the sombre hues of the conifers.

Right: Massed plantings of many-coloured rhododendrons seen across the lake studded with water lilies. Tall conifers give contrast of shape.

Sissinghurst Castle

In 1930 Sissinghurst Castle was derelict and was bought by the Hon. Sir Harold Nicolson and his wife, better known as Miss Victoria Sackville-West, the author. The rigid, formal garden plan was largely the work of Sir Harold; the planting, that of Miss Sackville-West. The partnership produced the subtle garden we now see, subtle in the grouping of plants, both for architectural form and colour. Particularly this is so in the white garden.

Dominated by a silvery, weeping, willow-leaved pear, with the woolly leaves of lamb's ears, white-flowered irises, and an occasional gigantic Scots thistle, it is a highly original composition. But there are vigorous colour schemes too, particularly the plantings involving the old shrub roses. The walls shelter many climbers – a famous plant, the rose 'Mme Alfred Carriere', covers an enormous space. There is a herb garden, an old-fashioned cottage garden, and a large rose garden. And everywhere, at all seasons of the year, there are flowers.

Sissinghurst Castle is half a mile off the A262, east of Sissinghurst village. The garden now belongs to the National Trust.

Overleaf: Formality of design combined with informality of planting makes Sissinghurst outstanding. The rigid, formal plan was largely the work of Sir Harold Nicolson, the planting that of his wife.

Below: The Herb Garden at Sissinghurst. The development of this garden into compartments has enabled a subtle development of architectural form and colour.

Stourhead

Stourhead was one of the first and still is one of the greatest landscape gardens in which the English threw off the fetters of Le Nôtre's French, rigid formality. Begun by the banker, Henry Hoare, after he inherited the property in 1741, the site was a bare, desolate valley with ponds in its bottom. The banks were planted with trees and the ponds were amalgamated and extended to make the present large lake. Around it a path was devised to provide a series of carefully contrived views, recalling the Italian landscapes painted by Claude in the seventeenth century, as well as incidents and events in classical authors such as Virgil.

The most important feature is the series of ornamental buildings, of the finest quality, most carefully contrived and placed (the architect Henry Flitcroft, whose principal work was Woburn Abbey, was closely concerned with these). These are no mere 'follies', but were full of significance to the Georgians, who were imbued with the classical spirit and had travelled the Grand Tour. There are temples, the Pantheon, the Temple of Flora and the Temple of Apollo, a fine grotto, a rock arch, a 'Gothick' cottage, well-heads and various bridges.

Above: The medieval Bristol High Cross at the entrance to the gardens. This was moved from Bristol to Stourhead in 1765.
Above left: The Palladian Bridge over an arm of the lake.
Left: Stourhead in spring with the rustic cottage and a profusion of rhododendrons in the foreground.

Above: Beside the lake stands the Pantheon, built in the mid-eighteenth century.

The subsequent history of the garden concerns its planting over the centuries with what were, at the time that they were put in, novelties. Many of these, particularly the conifers, are now outstanding specimens, while the massed plantings of rhododendrons and azaleas make a magnificent setting for the temples and other buildings, reflected as they are on a calm day of early summer in the lake. Later in the summer much colour is provided by hydrangeas, while in October the autumn colouring of the trees makes Stourhead well worth a visit.

Stourhead lies just off B3092 some nine miles south of Frome in Somerset, or, from Mere on the A303, a mile westward, then just over a mile northward of B3092.

Stowe

From the early years of the eighteenth century English garden makers were searching for a new style, less formal than the French, Italian and Dutch gardens then fashionable, and corresponding more closely to a romantic conception of nature. One of the leaders of the movement was William Kent. Stowe, Buckinghamshire, was his greatest creation. At Stowe, Kent worked with Charles Bridgeman, a formalist, from whom Kent eventually took over the designing of the garden. Kent developed to the full his ideas for a series of garden landscapes, each conceived as a picture much as an artist might conceive it. This was a period when dilettante interest in classical buildings was at its height, and Kent adorned his landscapes with temples, columns, statues and bridges in the classical manner. He swept away flower beds, parterres and formal pools, replacing them with grass following the natural contours of the land, with groups and belts of trees to open up the loveliest vistas and views of artificial lakes so cunningly formed that they appeared entirely natural.

Lancelot ('Capability') Brown, who was later to design so many English gardens, worked at Stowe under Kent. Many of the eighteenth century landscape gardens were later destroyed or greatly altered, but Stowe has remained largely untouched apart from the necessary replacement of trees.

Today Stowe is a great public school and its grounds must accommodate new buildings, playing fields, a golf course and facilities for sailing and rowing, but most of these do not noticeably detract from Kent's great design which remains as inspiring and as beautiful as ever.

Stowe is about three miles north of Buckingham. The gardens are open to the public in the afternoons at Easter and for a fortnight about the end of July.

Below: The Palladian Bridge at Stowe. Much of this garden was designed at a time when the interest in classical architecture was at its height and this is reflected in the many 'Classical' temples in the grounds.

Above: One approach to Stowe is by the Oxford Avenue, over the Oxford Bridge and between the Boycott Pavilions.

Right: The gothic temple, begun before 1744 built to an eccentric triangular plan, is an early gothic revival building.

Studley Royal

Studley Royal garden in Yorkshire is designed in the old formal architectural manner in a woodland setting of great picturesque beauty. Its origin is curious. John Aislabie, the owner of the estate, was Member of Parliament for nearby Ripon, becoming Chancellor of the Exchequer. He was involved in the 'South Sea Bubble' financial disaster, lost his office, narrowly escaped imprisonment, was fined £42,000, but remained well off, with his estates untouched. Presumably, as some consolation for his disgrace, in the valley of the little River Skill, he made this formal water garden, which has remained almost unchanged. It is approached from Ripon through a magnificent park. The design is entirely geometrical, the river itself is forced into a canal, and by its side are roughly circular-shaped pools overlooked by a Classically-styled temple. Standing by the temple, looking upstream, the valley seems blocked by trees. Following the path through their dense shade you come upon an unusual view. The river widens to form a small, half-moon shaped lake. Beyond it, as a terminating focal point, is a spectacular tower dominating the ruins of Fountains Abbey. The whole aspect of the place has been changed from formal to romantic and picturesque. The reason is that John Aislabie had always wished to acquire the upper part of the valley with its ruins but he was unable to do so. It was his son William, also an ardent garden designer, who obtained the property but in his time formality was out of fashion. There are several charming ornamental buildings, notably a banqueting house on the valley side.

The estate now belongs to the West Riding of York County Council, and is four miles south-west of Ripon and nine miles north of Harrogate.

Below: The little river Skell which runs through Studley Royal provides the water for the canal. This eventually runs over a weir and broadens out to become the River Skell again. The weir is flanked by rusticated piers and twin fishing lodges.

Right: Two of the pools, with the Temple of Piety beyond, on a slight rise and tucked into the wooded hillside.

Above: In the foreground is the lead statuary piece known as The Wrestlers in front of the long straight canal and in the distance, the Temple of Piety.

Right: Dominating the scene are the majestic ruins of the Cistercian monastery, founded in 1132 by thirteen Benedictine monks from York who joined the Cistercian Order.

Tintinhull

This Somerset garden, of no great size, but making use of modern ideas in planting, is a perfect example of early twentieth century simplicity and formality, with none of the over-elaborations typical of Victorian days. The key is set by the eighteenth century West front of the house, built of almost golden-coloured stone, from the neighbouring Ham quarries. It is symmetrical on either side of a round-arched portico, from which descend steps to ground level.

The main body of the garden is around either side of a walk, leading from this door, and at right angles to the house. Steps drop down to a flagged terrace, with a low balustrade in front. Against the house stand benches and plant-filled tubs. From this terrace runs a paved walk, the flagstones laid in a simple geometrical pattern. It goes straight until it ends in a dense wall of clipped yews, which, however, gives the hint that it divides and passes to either side. Throughout its length are placed low cones of clipped box to emphasize the direct lines as it goes through the small gardens that lie on either side. The first, the Eagle Court, is immediately below the house terrace and is a brick-walled, courtyard-like lawn, the path passing out of it through a wide opening, on either side of which eagles surmount pillars.

Another smaller lawn with wider beds follows. From it shallow steps lead through an opening into a paved enclosure of yew, in the centre of which is a lilypool. This terminates the main axis. Besides this long walk, there are areas divided by clipped hedges and linked by low flights of steps, so giving interest to a flat site. One encloses a narrow, canal-like pool with a loggia at the end; in another stands a many-limbed cedar. Great use is made of plants in tubs and large ornamental pots, in a variety of shapes.

Tintinhull House, a property of the National Trust, is five miles NW of Yeovil, a little south of A303. Dogs are not allowed on the property, but wheelchairs can be provided for disabled visitors.

Above: An attractive and highly fragrant combination of red roses and white regal lilies.

Left: The water in a sparsely planted formal pool reflects light and shadow. Groups of waterlilies lead the eye to the distant pergola.

Above: The small, late seventeenth-century manor house surrounded by a beautiful garden created by the late Mrs Reiss and donated by her to the National Trust in 1954.

Right: A formal paved area, relieved by ivy-leaved 'geraniums' planted in bold containers, leads on to the informal herbaceous border with an evergreen hedge background.

Wakehurst Place

Wakehurst Place, near Ardingly, Sussex, is an Elizabethan mansion built of local sandstone. It is situated on a narrow ridge of land with deep valleys to the west and east, which drain away much of the cold air when radiation frosts occur early in spring. Because of this it has been possible to grow many plants in the garden that would normally be considered too tender for this part of Britain and a truly magnificent collection has been built up in the past 60 years or so.

Much of the planting in the upper part of the garden follows the familiar glade style, with beds of irregular size and shape permanently planted with trees and shrubs, and separated by areas of mown grass. There is also an extensive heath garden in which the heathers are pleasantly and naturally associated with other shrubs, including brooms, which survive on acid soils and with a close covering of other plants.

There are several large lakes, the one nearest to the house being flanked by an exceptionally large and well-planted rock garden, in which Japanese maples are a feature. Rhododendrons also encircle this rock garden and a path leads on past fine plantations of hydrangeas, magnolias and azaleas for which Wakehurst Place is famous.

The path then continues past more lakes and down through rhododendron woods where even after the blaze of rhododendrons has died away, much quiet colour is provided by the tree foliage, to the Ardingly brook. Up the brook valley the more energetic visitor can return by a more circuitous route.

There is also an extensive pinetum on the high ground beyond the heather garden in which grows the lovely Mexican *Pinus patula* with slender drooping needles. The Sikkim larch, with hanging branchlets, and *Picea breweriana*, Brewer's Weeping Spruce, also grow there.

The gardens, now belonging to the National Trust, are used as an extension of the Royal Botanic Gardens, Kew.

Wakehurst lies one and a half miles north-west of Ardingly, Sussex, on the B2028 road.

Left: Some of the magnificent rhododendrons, camellias, acers, conifers and broad-leaved trees, for which Wakehurst Place is famous.

Overleaf: Autumn at Wakehurst Place can be one of the most colourful times of the year.

Weston Park

Turning off the roaring, crowded Watling Street, once a Roman road now a busy motor road, the visitor to Weston Park, Salop, soon finds himself winding through one of 'Capability' Brown's finest landscapes. The beautiful Restoration house, remarkable in that it was designed by its first owner, Lady Wilbraham, stands on a terraced garden. The broad, shallow terraces are decorated with topiary and ornamental vases. The final terrace takes the form of a balustraded arc, and on it grows an Oriental Plane, planted at least three centuries ago. Some 70 feet high, the branches spread over a circumference of 130 yards. From the terraces the view lies over the park to a typical 'Capability' Brown lake disappearing among trees.

A fine walk can be had by sauntering through the long, narrow Temple Wood. Through it wind paths bordered by rhododendrons, azaleas and flowering shrubs above which rise magnificent chestnuts, oaks and pines, terminating at one of the finest pieces of English garden architecture, James Gibb's Temple of Diana. Within are an orangery, tea room and music room. Beyond this are the long, narrow Temple Pool and Gibb's exquisite Roman bridge.

Nearer the house, the greenhouses and kitchen gardens will interest the practical gardener. The superb produce is grown by the organic method.

Weston Park is on the south of the A5 road at Weston-under-Lizard, five miles from Shifnal, 12 miles from Wolverhampton and 20 from Shrewsbury.

Below: Standing on the terraced garden the fine Restoration house at Weston Park, designed by Lady Wilbraham.

Right: The Oriental Plane planted three centuries ago, today stands some 70 feet high.

Below: Lawn and rhododendron groves.
Below right: Formality was added to the house at a later date.

Westonbirt Arboretum

Westonbirt Arboretum, Gloucestershire, is not just a scientific collection of trees but an enchanting garden of ornamental woodland, interplanted with innumerable shrubs. At every season of the year it has interest for the visitor, ranging from the spectacular effect of the giant conifers, including some of the biggest in Britain, to the smaller trees and rare shrubs from all parts of the world.

In winter, for contrast, there are the brilliant red boles of the large sequoias, the dazzling white bark of birches and winter-flowering cherries. From spring into summer, for unusual and often dazzling colour, there are the brilliant blossoms of azaleas, rhododendrons, magnolias and cherries, and any number of rarities, such as the Pyrenean oak with its grey and gold catkins.

The most popular season is generally mid-October, when the old and the new glades of maples are bathed in red and golden autumn tints.

Having soil that includes an area in which lime-hating plants such as rho-dodendrons will thrive set among ground that suits the lime-lovers, the arboretum has a bigger variety of trees and shrubs than any tree collection in the British Isles and rarities are clearly labelled. When it was begun by Robert Holford in 1829, he laid out the ground in curving rides and broad, straight avenues so that all his trees were shown to their best effect. This policy has been followed by his successors with equal success and is now continued by the Forestry Commission, who took over the arboretum in 1956.

There are two distinct areas. On approaching the car park that to the immediate right, covering 116 acres, contains the more spectacular plantings such as the maple glades, while down a bank to the left, in Silk Wood there are 45 acres of developed arboretum.

Westonbirt Arboretum lies three miles to the south-west of Tetbury, on the A433 road to Bath.

Below left: Rhododendrons thrive at Westonbirt and add spring colour to the arboretum.
Below: Birches and conifers in Silk Wood, where the trees can best be viewed by following the main path.

Above right: In autumn the bright tints of the fading leaves contrast brilliantly with the evergreens.
Above: A group of Lobocendrus in the arboretum.

Right: Acer Glade, an area planted with maples.

Windsor

The Savill Garden was started in 1932 as a water and bog garden around one of the smaller ponds in Windsor Great Park, Berkshire. Since the garden was started it has steadily grown and now covers over twenty acres. It includes many plants popular with modern gardeners. There are some particularly fine herbaceous borders, as well as rose gardens, raised beds for rock plants, shrub borders and climbers. Although it lacks the architectural interest of a fine house, the Savill garden is nevertheless of great interest and was created by Sir Eric Savill, deputy ranger of Windsor Great Park.

For instance, a wild woodland garden of great beauty has been made in the outlying parts of the garden, and further gardens have been added to the south in the direction of Virginia Water, the largest of the lakes in the park. The original bog garden now includes another large pond specially dug to show the interest of this type of garden. A wall built of old brick provides support for climbing plants. Further features of the park include the Punch Bowl, a natural amphitheatre filled with evergreen azaleas and Japanese maples, a heather garden, a valley of deciduous azaleas and the Valley Garden, beautifully landscaped.

The Savill Garden, which is Crown property, is reached from Wick Lane via Englefield Green from the A30 road.

Below: Spring in the Saville Garden, Windsor.
Below right: The azaleas in the natural amphitheatre called the Punch Bowl.

Above: The woodland forms the background to the azaleas and shrubs.

Right: The flowering cherries in spring are a delightful feature of the garden.
Far right: An attractive combination of water and mature lakeside trees.

Right: The Saville Garden is a water and bog garden built around a lake.

Winkworth

The site of this fine tree collection in Surrey, made entirely in the present century, could hardly be bettered on a hillside curling around a large lake. Surrounded by sheltering plantations of native trees and conifers with bluebells each spring, the arboretum has been steadily extended over the years and planting continues at the present time. Though the arboretum is not formal in design, there is a pleasant diversity in the planting, some of the trees and shrubs being placed as isolated specimens, some in groups, yet others in dense plantations with wonderful autumn colour. Paths of grass or beaten soil lead down from the car park at the top of the hillside to the lower level, through a glade of azaleas which are at their best in May and a wider path follows roughly the line of the lake. There are long vistas through the trees and more open glades, but the finest comprehensive view of the arboretum is to be obtained from the far side of the lake, where there is also a car park and an alternative approach.

Cedars and Blue spruces are particularly well placed, and there is a fine collection of Mountain ash, or Sorbus, and a great many maples and sumachs for brilliant autumn leaf. Cotoneasters produce berries freely and continue their display far into the winter. Hydrangeas for late summer colour are also a feature at Winkworth; indeed this is an arboretum which can be visited with pleasure at any time of the year.

Winkworth, owned by the National Trust, is about two miles south of Godalming.

Below: Winkworth Aboretum is worth a visit at any time of the year, but is particularly beautiful at bluebell time.

Right: Some of the wide variety of maples.

Below: Japanese maples, azaleas, and, behind, larches, Douglas firs and other conifers.

Wisley

In 1878 G. F. Wilson, an amateur gardener, bought an estate of derelict woodland at Wisley in Surrey. He opened clearings, made paths and ponds, and naturalised rhododendrons, lilies, irises and many other plants. After his death in 1902 this pioneer woodland garden was given in trust to the Royal Horticultural Society. Now extended to some 150 acres, practically every kind of gardening, ornamental and utilitarian, possible in Britain is displayed and studied. Near the entrance are the laboratories against whose sheltered walls tender plants are grown. Nearby are lawns with seasonally planted beds. Ahead is the range of glass houses, running due west, sheltering plants that range from the barely tender to tropical orchids.

To their south lie the mixed borders where shrubs and other plants are grown together in a practical arrangement. During the summer, the rose garden westward of this should be visited: through this are the fruit gardens.

Particularly in spring and early summer the wide grass path through the mixed borders should be followed up hill. It passes through massed azaleas and rhododendrons. To its left lies Battlestone Hill with paths winding among camellias, rhododendrons and similar shrubs. To the right of the broad walk are ornamental cherries.

The alpine meadow (with masses of tiny daffodils in spring), the world famous rock garden and the wild garden are reached by proceeding due west along the line of glass houses. From the wild garden the heath garden lies to the north-west. This merges with Seven Acres, a spacious planting of trees and shrubs around a large pool.

The long herbaceous borders (with the trials gardens on their left) are seen half-right from the laboratory. At their end, Seven Acres lies to the left and the large pinetum – a collection of conifers – to the right. Through this is Howard's Field, an example of planting on extremely dry, sandy soil that cannot be watered.

The gardens lie just off the A3 between Ripley and Cobham, 20 miles from London. Green Line Coach 715 runs within five minutes walk, taking about one hour 20 minutes from London. Enquire times from London Transport Executive.

Left: A stream meanders through the rock garden, ablaze with spring colour.

Above: A view of the Royal Horticultural Society's wild garden in Surrey. In such a natural, labour-saving setting, many plants such as primulas, lilies and ferns flourish.

Right: A view of the alpine meadow and rock garden from the wild garden. Primulas and bog plants flourish by the stream.

Wrest Park

The present house at Wrest Park, Bedfordshire, was built in an ornate French style early in the last century. The level garden viewed from the terrace was begun in 1706 and altered several times afterwards to fit in with changing fashions.

Immediately in front of the terrace are colourful parterre beds and an ornate marble fountain in the French style. In the distance across lawns, can be seen the Long Water, an original feature, which is a straight, formal canal between high trees with a domed pavilion at one end. The best introduction to the garden is first to walk down to this attractive building. It was planned by William Archer, who also designed the monumental cascade pavilion at Chatsworth, Derbyshire. The pavilion at Wrest Park is decorated inside with trompe l'oeil work, consisting of figures and architectural decorations painted on the flat but made to appear quite solid-looking.

Entrances to a surrounding wood lead away from the canal. The wood contains a complex network of paths arranged for the most part geometrically, but including many that meander in an almost maze-like and apparently aimless way. By following them, all kinds of interesting discoveries are made. One terminates at a Roman altar, another with a vase. A third ends at a small summer-house, others lead to monuments. Emerging into the open, stretches of water come into view – a narrow, irregular lake surrounds the whole woodland area. In one place it is crossed by a Chinese-style bridge built in 1874.

Nearer the house is a handsome Palladian bowling-green pavilion made in 1735, a fine orangery in the French manner built in 1836 and a rustic bath house and late eighteenth-century bridge.

Wrest Park, now the property of the National Institute of Agricultural Engineering, is at Silsoe, ten miles north of Luton on the A6 Bedford Road.

Left: The bath house, recently restored, stands in a secluded part of the garden at Wrest Park.

Right: The formal canal with the pavilion beyond forms the access to the garden.

Below: The parterre with the orangery and the bowling-green pavilion beyond stress the formality of this section of the garden.

Picture credits

Aerofilms: 72TL; Amateur Gardening: 116; P. Ayres: 77 (2 pics); 78; 92; D. Baker: 3tr; Belton House Estate; 21c; D. Blogg: 103; G. W. Bolton: 59; 60 (2 pics); 67r; 68br; 73tl; 78; 80b; P. Booth: 124b; 126bl; British Tourist Authority: 27bl; 28; 36tr; 45r; 46r; 55; 71; 112br; 117; Clark Nelson Ltd.: 94t; V. Finnis: 61l; 63; 64 (3 pics); 113r; 114t; 122t; M. Hadfield: 11bl; 12bl; G. Hall: 71; I. Hardwick: 6; 23; 24 (2 pics); 37bl; 38 (2 pics); 39; 40bl; 43 (2 pics); 44; 53; 54tr; 56; 57 (2 pics); 58 (2 pics); 61bl; 62; 80tr; 81 (2 pics); 84 (3 pics); 85; 86 (3 pics); 92; A. Hellyer: 11br; 12tr; 29; 30tr; 31; 35 (2 pics); 36b; 41; 42br; 65r; 87; 88t; 97bl; 98 (2 pics); 99 (2 pics); 100b; 111; 121 (2 pics); 122 (3 pics); M. Holford: 2; P. Hunt: 13 (2 pics); 14 (3 pics); 21 (2 pics); 22; 26; 27bl; 32 (3 pics); 47; 48 (2 pics); 49 (2 pics); 50; 65bl; 66 (3 pics); 67bl; 68 (2 pics); 109; 110 (2 pics); 112l; 113bl; 114bl; A. J. Huxley: 7; 76tr; 90tr; 108; A. Kersting: 51; 69; 83; 90b; 104; 107 (3 pics); 123; 124tr; K. Lemmon: 112tr; C. Lines: 40t; 100tr; 118 (2 pics); P. Minay: 70 (3 pics); S. J. Orme: 30 (2 pics); 95; 96 (2 pics); D. Pearce: 119bl; 120tr; Picturepoint: 8; 9; 10 (3 pics); 45bl; 46br; 73br; 74; 75; 76 (2 pics); 88br; 101bl; 102; Popperfoto: 25br; Ministry of Public Buildings & Works: 128b; A. de Rahm: 25bl; 54b; 91 (2 pics); 106; I. Ruthven: 19; 20 (3 pics); K. Sanecki: 15 (2 pics); 16; 17 (2 pics); 18 (2 pics); 42t; Scala: 3tl; A. Schilling: 115; D. Smith: 5; 127; 128tr; H. Smith: 33; 34 (2 pics); 61r; 82 (2 pics); 93bl; 97br; 101br; 105; 120br; 125b; G. Thomas: 52 (2 pics); 89; D. Thornely: 93 (2 pics); 94br; J. Treasure: 37 (2 pics); B. Unne: 72b; T. Wright: 119br; 120tl;